She Who Prays

She Who Prays

A WOMAN'S INTERFAITH PRAYER BOOK

Jane Richardson Jensen
and
Patricia Harris-Watkins

morehouse

HARRISBURG • LONDON

Morehouse Publishing, P.O. Box 1321, Harrisburg, PA 17105
Morehouse Publishing, The Tower Building, 11 York Road, London SE1 7NX
Morehouse Publishing is a Continuum imprint.

Cover Design: Laurie Westhafer

Library of Congress Cataloging-in-Publication Data

Jensen, Jane Richardson.
She who prays : a woman's interfaith prayer book / Jane Richardson Jensen and Patricia Harris-Watkins.
p. cm.
Includes bibliographical references.
ISBN 0-8192-2113-9 (pbk.)
1. Women—Prayer-books and devotions—English. I. Harris-Watkins, Patricia. II. Title.
BL625.7.J46 2005
242'.843—dc22

2004010699

Printed in the United States of America

05 06 07 08 09 10 9 8 7 6 5 4 3 2 1

To the Glory of God

Jane gives thanks for
her Mother,
Martha Gates Richardson,
A Woman of Prayer,
and for
Irving, Rosemary, and Richard who
planted, watered, and fertilized the seeds of creativity
that blossomed into this book.

Patricia gives thanks for
the Strong Women in her life:
Alison, Heather, Logan Emily, and Natalie Elisabeth,
and for Charlie,
brother, husband, and father of the Strong Women.

CONTENTS

ACKNOWLEDGMENTS

Jane Richardson Jensen would like to applaud Patricia Harris-Watkins, without whose good-natured yet truthful mentoring this book would be but a shadow of what it has become.

Jane would also like to recognize Diane Owen Johnson for her creative vision and generosity in sharing her expertise in computer skills; Deborah Lansley and Charlene Cobb for their encouragement and spiritual support; and Leanne, Cathy, and Jerry Jensen for listening and sharing their unique gifts. Leanne offered artistic insights and ideas about great women; Cathy encouraged Jane to trust herself about using a variety of prayers, and Jerry shared his experiences and enthusiasm for engaging in creative pursuits—even if it meant Jane's typing late into the night. To all of the above, thank you.

Patricia Harris-Watkins appreciates Jane Jensen's diligence and inspired creativity. She also gives thanks for her prayer partner, Gail Ostensen, and her willingness to explore Native American spirituality. In addition, Patricia would like to honor the memory of her colleagues and teachers, Mary Whitten and Mary Agnes Taylor. She sends a voice of thanksgiving honoring her grandmothers, Tama and Leatha, and her mother Flossie. Most of all, Patricia honors life lessons learned from her friend and teacher, Glenda Little Hawk Taylor, as well as from her husband, George H. Watkins, Jr.

Patricia and Jane would also like to thank their editor, Nancy Fitzgerald, for her enthusiasm and timely responses. Her willingness to work with us on last-minute changes has been a blessing.

IN A NUTSHELL

Hi! You're invited
to take time for yourself, to try something new.
When I'm asked to do something I haven't done before,
I like to know
what to expect, how to dress, what to bring, and who'll be there.
Here's what you need to know to incorporate these prayers into your spiritual journey.

What to expect:
Basic services for the usual times people are likely to pray every day—
at the start of the day, on a lunch break, or at the end of the day.
Six unique services for sharing with a group.
Suggestions called rubrics—in italics *like this*—to help the services flow smoothly.
If you're praying a service by yourself,
you may want to read one part silently and the other out loud.

How to dress:
Comfortably.
The services are arranged for those who enjoy the coziness of
a traditional prayer book pattern,
but would prefer a church calendar, readings, and prayers that are
woman-friendly and respectful of other faiths.

What to bring:
Yourself and an openness to the Open-Handed One!
Whether these services are for your own private use or for a group,
let the Spirit lead you.

Who'll be there:

The Divine Mystery and thee,
the communion of saints, and any animal, plant, mineral, or person you invite.

This book offers words of contemplation, comfort, challenge, compassion, and confidence.
May it enrich your special time with God.

ENTRYWAY: GUIDELINES FOR THE READER

We hope you've already picked up this book and thumbed through it a bit, maybe even taken the time to glance at a few of the prayers. This isn't a novel or a textbook, so it's not meant to be read from cover to cover. This book is divided into six parts to offer you the variety of a smorgasbord. You might choose your dessert first, then choose your entrée, and finish off with a salad. The tables in Part Six are truly the icing on the cake. Since they make the meal richer and sweeter, we encourage you to glance through these early on.

We hope this book will be a feast for your soul. So we'd like to acquaint you with the layout of the book, to show you the floor plan of this banquet hall you're about to enter. We begin our tour at the entryway. Like an entryway to a house, this chapter is the doorway to the prayer book. We hope you'll enjoy browsing through it as you would if you were standing in an intriguing entryway filled with artwork, statuary, and flowers. Like the entryway, this book is a collage of writings by different authors, all ancient except for Jim Cotter's Alternative Lord's Prayer and our own prayers.

When you walk through the doorway into the banquet hall, the first thing that catches your eye is a large table. It's big enough to allow for different kinds of dining experiences—from Sunday brunch to Wednesday takeout to Thanksgiving dinner—yet still be comfortable.

The table is **Part One: One-Week Cycle of Daily Prayer,** and it is set for a week's feast of prayers for morning, midday, and evening. But the days' names aren't the usual Sunday, Monday, and so on. Instead, we've returned to the original meanings of the names of the days. This enabled us to discern a theme for each day, either one that supports the day's significance or one that counters it. The days of the week and their themes are:

First Day, Day of the Sun: Light and Joy
Second Day, Day of the Moon: Darkness and Hidden-ness
Third Day, Day of Tiw: Peace
Fourth Day, Day of Wodin: Wisdom
Fifth Day, Day of Thonar: Thunder and Sky
Sixth Day, Day of Freya: Love
Seventh Day, Day of Saturn: Sowing Seed

Just as the earth and sky change, so you are a slightly different person in the morning or at night, from one day to the next. So picture yourself sitting in different places around the table to represent the cosmic and personal cycles of life. There's still enough of a connection to our regular weekdays to avoid confusion, but also the freedom to choose a theme you'd like for your day. Those who do shift work may more easily start the cycle on the First Day, regardless of what their first workday is. The reader doesn't need to stick rigidly to a Sunday–Saturday week, or to a Monday–Sunday one either.

Now for more about what you'll find on the banquet table of Daily Prayer. First, there are actually very few readings from the Bible in deference to people of faith who are uncomfortable with the male-oriented and militaristic nature of the Bible, or to those who have been hurt by their religious traditions. The biblical readings are taken primarily from the Wisdom literature of the Apocrypha. Apocrypha is a Greek word that means "hidden things." It is used for a group of books or parts of books that are now known as Deuterocanonical Scripture by the Roman Catholic, Greek, and Russian Orthodox churches. They are also called the Deuterocanonical Books of the Old Testament. They were part of the Greek Septuagint of the Jewish Community in Alexandria, Egypt from which the Latin Vulgate was translated. But they were not in the Hebrew Masoretic Text of Palestine, so versions of the Bible that were translated strictly from the Hebrew do not have them at all. Lutherans and other reformed churches include the Apocrypha in a separate section. These churches consider the Apocrypha good reading, but not Holy Scripture.[1]

For other readings, we're using excerpts from the *Mekhilta of Rabbi Ishmael,* the *Odes of Solomon,* the *Acts of Judas Thomas,* the *Macarian Homilies,* and the *Hymns of St. Ephrem the Syrian.* The *Mekhilta of Rabbi Ishmael* is typically described as a *halakhic midrash,* or legal interpretation, of Exodus, beginning with chapter 20. It was written in Hebrew and has been dated from the end of the fourth until as late as the eighth century.[2] The excerpt from the *Mekhilta* is about the universality of God's gifts.

Except for the *Mekhilta,* the rest of the sources are Syrian, which means, despite their language of preservation or origin, they were written in the region of northern Mesopotamia and its eastern neighbor, Adiabene, now southern Turkey.[3] The language Syriac, however, is more encompassing. After Greek and Latin, Syriac—the Eastern, or Christian, dialect of Aramaic—was the third international language of the early church. Besides being the language of communication in Syria, Palestine, and Mesopotamia, it was the language missionaries used to spread the Gospel to Persia (Iran), Armenia, Georgia, India, and Ethiopia.[4]

The *Odes of Solomon,* a collection of early second-century writings, has been preserved in Syriac, Greek, and Coptic manuscripts. The *Acts of Judas Thomas* are usually supposed to have been written in Syriac in the region of Northern Mesopotamia, possibly Edessa in Southern Turkey sometime between about 200 and 225. The Greek version is called the *Acts of Thomas.* The *Acts* claim to relate the teachings of Jesus as spoken through the apostle Thomas, the "twin brother of Christ." The names Judas (Greek, *didymus*) and Thomas (Syriac, *tauma*) both mean "twin." The *Macarian Homilies* were, at first, thought to be the work of Macarius of Egypt (300–390). But they now seem more likely to be the work of Symeon of Mesopotamia, so we date them to the fourth or fifth century.[5] Though the homilies were written in Greek, they were soon translated into Syriac. The Syrian texts present either God the Father or the Holy Spirit as a nurturing Mother.

The majority of the readings in the Weekly Cycle of Daily Prayer are taken from the hymns of a fourth-century church father, St. Ephrem the Syrian, a deacon and a poet also known as St. Ephraim of Edessa (Edessa is near the Syrian border). Ephrem and his parishioners were extremely well versed in the Bible, so the subjects of his hymns are biblical, but with a twist. Ephrem had an exciting visionary perspective of faith and a sacramental theology, which means he saw God in all of creation. He used feminine images for God and affirmed women in his writings. In fact, he wrote hymns for women's choirs. One of the foremost theologians of the Syrian or Eastern churches that encompass the Assyrian (or Nestorian) Church of the East, the Syrian Orthodox, the Syro-Malabar, and Syro-Malankara Churches in India (usually called "Mar Thomas Christians"), the Maronite, the Chaldean, and the Syrian Catholic Church, he is also recognized as a Doctor of the Church, or Teacher of the Faith, in western liturgical traditions (the Roman Catholic Church and the churches of the Anglican Communion). (The Eastern churches still exist, though they are small in number.)

St. Ephrem, whose sacramental theology supports our concerns for the environment and whose hymns suggest an ability to identify with women, is becoming popular again today as people of faith realize that valuing both sexes enables women and men to use their full range of gifts. As females integrate the masculine mode of existence, and males their feminine mode, "each becomes whole but not the same, alike but not identical."[6] Some of Ephrem's feminine imagery may be accounted for by the possibility that he was receptive to his feminine side. While he preferred virginity and celibacy, he still valued marriage and children. The Syriac-speaking church clearly developed at a different pace and in other directions than the Greek-speaking church. Almost without exception, Ephrem used feminine imagery to build up the women and men in his church.

Ephrem is most well known for his *madrashe,* of which over 400 have been preserved. The word *madrash* is derived from the Syriac root *d.r.sh.,* which means "to expound, preach, search out." *Madrash,* which corresponds to the Hebrew *midrash,* also means hymn. (The Islamic religious schools we've heard so much about since 9/11 are called *madrassas*; their name comes from the same root in Arabic.) Since Ephrem wrote his *madrashe* in verse and gave the melody to which they were to be sung, they are usually called hymns, although unfortunately the musical accompaniment has been lost.

Incorporating excerpts from Ephrem's hymns into services in a prayer book is a departure from the usual practice of publishing translations of his hymns in scholarly editions that are mainly for specialists. Jane is happy to introduce you to a church father whose pastoral sensitivity pastored her through infertility treatments and healed some of the misogynistic wounds she picked up earlier from reading certain Greek and Latin church fathers.

The English translations of these Hebrew, Greek, and Syriac sources are Jane's. They are intended to be dynamic, easily readable translations. But translating is not an exact science. For example, the letter *b* in English corresponds to *beth,* the second letter of the Syriac, Aramaic, Hebrew, and Arabic alphabets. It can be translated as "in, among, with, at, to, into, on, upon, by, according to, for, because, about," and occasionally as "through."[7] To see what impact a translator's word choice can have on a translation, you only need to think about the Hebrew word *adam,* in Genesis 1:26, which is usually translated as "man." However, *adam* can also mean "human" or "humanity." Translating *adam* as "human" helps us understand humanity's closeness to the earth, *adamah,* from which the first human came (Genesis 2). Since Genesis 1:26–27 says that humans were created male and female in the image of God, "human" really is the more correct translation. This word choice also leads to a fuller vision of God who has both masculine and feminine aspects.

For Jane's translations of St. Ephrem's hymns, she used the Syriac texts in the volumes edited by Dom Edmund Beck in the *Corpus Scriptorum Christianorum Orientalium* (*C.S.C.O.*), the most readily available source of the Syriac versions.[8] The pronouns in Jane's translations correspond to the Syriac forms used by Ephrem, which generally mean "She" for the Spirit and the Word, because *ruach* and *mellta* are grammatically feminine. Using "She" for the Holy Spirit is also more expressive of the nuances in the Semitic milieu from which Christianity came. The relations of grammatical and metaphorical gender to biological sex are of interest because femininity and masculinity are matters of sexuality as much as of gender. A fuller understanding of sexuality enables people to express and experience their humanity in ways that encourage community and diminish alienation.

Valuing faiths besides our own is another way of strengthening community and reducing alienation. To show respect for followers of other faiths we capitalize the names of all religions (for example, Zoroastrianism) and groups within a given religion (Sufis). We follow the traditional practice of capitalizing the names of animals and other references to concepts in Native American Spirituality, such as Turtle and Mother Earth. It's a matter of showing respect when the words denote either the teacher aspect of a being (Song of the Trees, Wolf who teaches us about family), or when the closeness of a relative is implied (Grandfather Sun, Sister Bear). We've also capitalized the first letter of words when they are divine attributes (Spirit, Word, Light, and so on).

In appreciation of women whose words were too often left unrecorded or were lost or destroyed, Jane has written songs for two women who are known because their images and functions were preserved. They are "She-Who-Beholds-the-Beauty-of-her-Lord," who is depicted on a funerary epithet and "She-Who-Beats-the-Rhythm," whose image is titled the "Percussionist" of Meir from the Old Kingdom of Egypt (2686–2181 B.C.E.).[9]

We've also included an original "Song" each day during the weekly cycle of prayers in honor of a Mother Goddess. Out of the many possibilities, the ones we have chosen are Bast, the Egyptian Cat Goddess, for Sunday; Arianrhod, the Welsh Moon Goddess, for Monday; White Buffalo Calf Woman for Tuesday; Changing Woman for Wednesday; Pele, the Hawaiian Goddess of Volcanoes, for Thursday; Freya, the Norse Goddess of Love and Fertility, for Friday; and Spider Woman for Saturday. Jane wrote the ones for Bast, Arianrhod, and Freya, while Patricia wrote the songs for White Buffalo Calf Woman, Changing Woman, Pele, and Spider Woman. Although we both consider ourselves Christians, we included the Goddesses as a way of affirming the Divine Feminine. The Affirmation of Faith used in the Daily Cycle of Prayer is based on the Bible verses that underpinned the original core values for Clare's Place, a local women's support group at our church out of which the backbone of these prayers grew.

The special collection on display in the china cabinet is **Part Two: Season Stories and Collects for Each Week of the Year**. Patricia Harris-Watkins, who blends her Native American heritage with her Christian faith, has prayerfully and thoughtfully correlated the traditional meanings associated with the creatures, plants, and minerals in the Medicine Wheel to write her fifty-two Collects. Each Collect expresses a correspondence between a specific quality or attribute and an animal; in addition to this correspondence, the plant and the mineral that best matches the quality is listed before the Collect.

The set of three—animal, plant, and mineral—plus the human completes the four-part paradigm order of creation as seen in many Native American spiritual practices. Altars for private or for communal prayer, then, can be set up with a picture or figurine of the animal, a picture of or vase with the flower or plant, and a picture or specimen of the mineral.

Before writing the prayers, Patricia, with Jane's help, essentially did a fifty-two-card spread with Jamie Sams's Medicine Cards, separating the cards into four more or less equal piles. The cards were then arranged in a meaningful sequence of associations and connections to the seasons of the year and of human life and human spiritual evolution (spring/maid/beginner, summer/young matron/proficient, fall/adult/master, and winter/old age/wisdom teacher). The full-deck spread consisted of associating each animal with a particular season (and direction on the Medicine Wheel), then sequencing them in a narrative focused on a woman whose age paralleled the season—maid (spring), young matron (summer), woman in her prime (autumn), and elder (winter). Next, a narrative was constructed for a woman who was the epitome of the card qualities for each season. Part of the association process was seeing the story for each stage of woman's spiritual development with its theme of prayers and the sequence of the creatures' attributes. In doing the initial spread, Patricia omitted a few cards for personal preference and added a few from Ted Andrews's books because they were more personally meaningful to her after working with Sams's cards and Andrews's books for more than ten years. For cat lovers everywhere, Patricia included the cat and its typical characteristic—independence; blue jay was added because of its persistence. Some of the qualities of the animals were also shifted; for example, "weasel" became not "stealth," but "hunting," and "owl" not "deception" but "sharing." The animals, plants, and minerals and their associated qualities or attributes appear in a table in Part Six, for use in constructing a personal altar or in choosing a particular group to pray with for a time. If the weekly Collects are the everyday dishes from which we are nourished, then the Season Stories are the platters that hold our special family meals.

In the lower part of the china cabinet, tucked in the drawers and cupboards, is **Part Three: Prayers for Hearth and Home and Beyond**. Like the embroidered tablecloths or the silver candlesticks we bring out from time to time, this part offers prayers for some of the memorable times of a woman's life—times of giving, times of broken relationships, and times of healing. There are prayers also for those who feel like round people in square holes. The prayer, *For Times of War,* was written in response to September 11, 2001, to reconcile the hawks and the doves who were questioning what it means to be Christian in these circumstances. Please note these prayers are not autobiographical per se, but rather, we hope, appropriate for the occasional events—both ordinary and momentous—that women in general experience.

When you look at the opposite wall, you see a mirror, and a cookie jar on top of a silver chest on the wall reserved for **Part Four: Mystics, Saints, and Other Extraordinary Folk, Events, and Gifts of Creation**. You quickly realize the mirror's not an ordinary one—instead of your reflection, it offers a glimpse of your inner self as it reveals the lives of extraordinary people like you. This dazzling mirror tells you about the church calendar, explaining what it is and how to use it for your spiritual journey. Below the mirror, resting on a silver chest, is a cookie jar. Most of the names, events, or gifts of Creation (geomorphology is a fancy word for this) in this cookie-jar calendar have to do with the lives of women, or with simply being human. The geomorphological features (lakes, canyons, planets, and colors) are included to encourage people to take time to appreciate their surroundings. Each entry has enough information for you to be able to create your own prayer if you wish. But to help you along on a busy day, there are more than a hundred Collects (or prayers) ready to use. The entries on the calendar with an individual Collect are marked by a star (*). The multi-purpose Collects for a general subject, like landforms or planets, are marked by number sign (#). As you might expect, the silver chest holds the family treasures. These Collects make up the major part of Part Four. Whether you create your own Collect or use one of the designated Collects by a star or number sign, we pray you'll grow in grace through the experience.

Outside the banquet hall is a porch that goes around three sides of the house. This is where you'll find **Part Five: Rites, Rituals, and Services for Special Occasions**, important events that, like the porch, fall outside the realm of the ordinary regions of the house. The front porch contains the Service of Beginnings with two rituals, one for welcoming a new member into the family, the other for joining two individuals in a covenant relationship.

At the back of the hall is the kitchen with a well-stocked larder and an old-fashioned fireplace. Like the family kitchen that provides for our most basic need for nourishment, here you'll find A Rite to Redeem Eden's Goodness, an alternative Lord's Supper or Eucharist that can be led by anyone. It is a simple service of sharing, using water, a basic necessity for life, and an apple, a tangible image of creation because of the seeds in the core of the fruit. A kitchen door leads to the side porch, where two Services of Transformation take place. The first is A Service of Healing (on a small-scale or individual level). It was written especially for people, including our foremothers, who have suffered violence. A Service of Reconciliation (healing on a large-scale or global level) is also here. Here there are prayers for the followers of the world's religions and for living in harmony with creation. We hope the Service of Reconciliation helps decrease the alienation that some have experienced after 9/11/01 and strengthens a sense of community, especially among people of different faiths or traditions. We see Divinity as an orb or a sphere with individual religions as longitudes and denominations or branches within a given religion as latitudes. So the distinctions that divide religions are primarily on the surface (though deeply felt). But if you cut a slice out of the sphere, you move away from the divisions and draw closer to what religions have in common—the Divine core.[10] The Table of the Religions of the World at the back of the book gives some general information about fifteen religions. But there are so many religions and denominations or groups within the broad band of any given religion that we finally decided to focus on the religions that sent representatives to the Conference of the Earth's Community of Religions in 1995.[11] So Wicca is included, but none of the other neo-pagan groups are.[12]

The garden of the banquet hall is devoted to a Labyrinth Service. Although the Service can stand alone, it may be used as part of the Service of Reconciliation. In fact, it was first used to celebrate Earth Day 2000 to dedicate the outdoor Labyrinth at St. Francis Episcopal Church in College Station, Texas. While it is ideal for an Earth Day service, it maybe used at any time, for a permanent outdoor labyrinth or the indoor, movable kind.

The last area we'd like you to know about is the closet. Yes, you have permission to peek into the closets, and even into the spectacular chest, of this banquet hall. Tucked away in a large chest of drawers in the closet is **Part Six: About What's Inside**. Being familiar with these bits will help you get the most out of the services in this prayer book. The contents of the top drawer are especially for the public services. We have included instructions for making and using various crafts to bring the prayers to life. Like the bread and wine at Communion, the handcrafts give visual and physical expression to the concepts of the prayers. Drawer two has the table of associations listing the animal, plant, and mineral triads for the Collects for each week of the year, and drawer three has the Table of the Religions of the World, which has already been introduced. In drawer four there are lists of the original works written by Jane and Patricia for each part of the book. In drawer five, there is the Bibliography for Translations of the Works Cited from Ancient Sources. Drawer six is the General Bibliography, which includes the material used for the Table of the Religions and the material for the Collects and Correlations. The bottom drawer has the Bibliography for the People and Events on the Church Calendar.

Now that you've found your way around, relax for a while. Bon appetit! Enjoy this feast for your soul! Enjoy being She Who Prays!

NOTES

1. John Bowker, ed., *The Oxford Dictionary of World Religions* (Oxford, N.Y.: Oxford University Press, 1997), 80–81.

2. Bowker, 632. For more detail and the Hebrew text, see Jane E. Richardson, "*Mekhilta of Rabbi Ishmael's Bahodesh* 5–8 (The Ten Commandments)." (master's thesis, University of Texas at Austin, December 1985), 8–9, 43 (5.IX). The excerpt is *Bahodesh* 5.98b–100 in Jacob Z. Lauterbach, *Mekilta de-Rabbi Ishmael.* II. (1933; repr., Philadelphia: The Jewish Publication Society of America, 1976), 237.

3. For information on St. Ephrem the Syrian, the *Odes of Solomon,* the *Macarian Homilies,* and the *Acts of Judas Thomas,* see Jane Richardson Jensen, "Father, Son, and Holy Spirit as Mothers in Early Syrian Literature," *Continuum* 2, nos. 2 and 3 (1993): 27–49. For the Syriac with Edmund Beck's German translation and critical notes, see the *Corpus Scriptorum Christianorum Orientalium* (Louvain, Belgium):

Hymnen De Fide, Vol. 154, Scriptores Syri 73 (1955)
Hymnen De Nativitate, Vol. 186, Scriptores Syri 82 (1959)
Hymnen De Eccelsia, Vol. 198, Scriptores Syri 84 (1960)
Carmina Nisibena, Vol. 218, Scriptores Syri 92 (1961)
Hymnen De Virginitate, Vol. 23, Scriptores Syri 94 (1962)
Paschahymnen (De Resurrectione), Vol. 248, Scriptores Syri 108 (1964)
Sermo De Domino Nostro, Vol. 270, Scriptores Syri 116 (1966).

4. John Meyendorff, "Preface" in Susan McVey, *St. Ephrem the Syrian Hymns* (Mahwah, N.Y.: Paulist Press, 1989), 1.

5. Heinz Berthold, ed., *Reden und Briefe (von) Makarios/Symeon. Die Sammlung I des Vaticanus Graecus 694 (B)* (Berlin: Verlag, 1973), ix.

6. William F. Kraft, *Sexual Dimensions of the Celibate* (Dublin: Gill & Macmillan, 1979), 39.

7. Francis Brown, S. R. Driver, and Charles A. Briggs, *A Hebrew and English Lexicon of the Old Testament.* (1906; repr., Oxford: Clarendon Press, 1951), 88–91; and J. Payne Smith (Mrs. Margoliouth), ed., *A Compendious Syriac Dictionary: Founded upon the Thesaurus Syriacus of R. Payne Smith.* (1903; repr., Oxford: Clarendon Press, 1985), 33.

8. Ephrem's hymns will be referred to by the title hymn number and stanza numbers. The full references for St. Ephrem's hymns are in the Bibliography.

9. Barbara S. Lesko, ed., *Women's Earliest Records From Ancient Egypt and Western Asia* (Atlanta: Scholars Press, 1989), 6, 18.

10. Frithjof Schuon, *The Transcendent Unity of Religions,* rev. ed. (Wheaton, Ill.: Theosophical Publishing, 1993), xii.

11. Joel Beversluis, ed., *A Sourcebook for Earth's Community of Religions,* rev. ed. (Grand Rapids, Mich.: CoNexus Press with Global Education Associates, 1995).

12. For a wide-ranging discussion of Wicca and neo-pagan religions/groups, see Margot Adler, *Drawing Down the Moon,* rev. ed. (1979; repr., New York: Penguin Compass, 1986).

PART ONE

One-Week Cycle of Daily Prayer

The Banquet Table

Welcome to the dining room. The banquet table has twenty-one place settings with services for morning, midday, and evening prayer. That's enough to feast your soul for a full week! So as if you were at a smorgasbord, look around the table to see what's here. Then choose a day or theme, and morning, midday, or evening, get comfortable, and tuck in. You are already becoming She Who Prays!

If you are praying any of the daily services alone, try reading the plain print silently and the bold print, when it appears, out loud. If two or more are gathered together for a daily service, you may take turns reading the prayers.

FIRST DAY, DAY OF THE SUN: LIGHT AND JOY

Morning Prayer

Greeting

The Mother of the saints rejoices and is glad.
Macarian Homily 27

THE FIRST DAY

In the beginning when God created the heavens and the earth, the earth was a formless void and darkness covered the face of the deep, while a wind from God swept over the face of the waters. Then God said, "Let there be light";

and there was light. And God saw the light was good; and God separated the light from the darkness. God called the light Day, and the darkness he called Night. And there was evening and there was morning, the first day.

GENESIS 1:1–5

COLLECT FOR MORNING

Morning Star, as the sun moves through the heavens, night becomes day. As the Spirit moves through the world, the dusks and dawns of life become holy ground. May I feel the sparkle of your radiance so deeply within, that I am able to live fully into this day. Let my spirit play in your presence, regardless of what transpires. For I pray in the name of the Sacred Three. Amen.

Prayers

Offer Personal Prayers and Thanksgiving.
Choose Collects from Parts Two, Three, or Four, as desired.

JESUS, THE LIVING BREAST

Jesus lay down and sucked Mary's milk, and all creation sucks from his goodness.
He is the Living Breast.
The dead sucked living breath from his life and lived.
While indeed he sucked Mary's milk, he suckled the living—every one.
While again he rests in his mother's womb, all of creation rests in his womb.

ST. EPHREM THE SYRIAN'S *HYMNS OF NATIVITY 4.149–150, 153–54*

SONG OF BAST

I am Mau, the Mother, the great cat of Egypt.
I give light and life, and independence, too.
Though I can be wild, I can also be tender as
I care for mothers in childbirth.
Mothering takes time, both inside the womb and out.
Being a good mother means taking time to play.
Celebrate new life with me.
Dance in the beginning of a new week with me.
Rejoice in your relationships and in your independence.

AN AFFIRMATION OF FAITH

I believe that you, O God, created humanity, female and male, in your image.
I hear you, O Lord, and your call to love you with all my heart, with all my soul, with all my strength, and with all my mind, and your command to love my neighbors as myself.

I accept others, just as you have accepted me, in order to bring praise to you, O God.
I hope to shine like the stars in the universe as I hold out the word of life to my community.
I am committed to growing in your knowledge and love and to participating in the life of my faith community.
I praise you for removing my sackcloth and clothing me with yourself so that my heart may sing to you and not be silent.
I hope through Jesus the Risen One in the power of the Holy Spirit now and forever. Amen.

BASED ON GENESIS 1:26, MARK 12:29-31, ROMANS 15:7, PHILIPPIANS 2:15, ACTS 2:42, AND PSALMS 30:11-12.

Closing

May the Light who lightens my life today illumine all of my tomorrows!

Midday Prayer

Greeting

Delight of my heart, rest in my peace; nestle into my presence.

AL-'ASMA' AL-HUSNA, "THE BEAUTIFUL NAMES"

Holy One of One-Hundred Beautiful Names,
three of which are Compassion, Love, and Mercy,
I acknowledge my offenses against you and your creation.
In my attempts to be holy, too often I have listened to others
instead of trusting my own God-given instincts.
I have accepted distorted images of women for so long
that I no longer recognize the godly goodness of my own voice.
I have tarnished the unique God-shaped image that you so tenderly created inside
each one of us, female and male.
I confess the times I have not loved you, Creation, my neighbors, or myself.
I am rarely able to receive your all-encompassing love.
Instead of fanning the flames of your love in my midst, too often I have quenched the divine sparks.
Instead of allowing your Holy Breath to swirl around me freely, sometimes
I have tried to trap the breeze in a box to be used for my own purposes.

I ask you to blow away the cobwebs of temptation and to blot out the stain of my offenses.
I pray that your light may shine through me, and I may become all you created me to be.
I hope that I may reflect your Glorious Harmony in the world.
I ask this in your Beautiful Names, O God of One Hundred Names, but especially in the name of Jesus through the power of the Holy Spirit. Amen.

COLLECT FOR MIDDAY

Holy Mystery, you are the life force that courses through my soul. When my world is spinning like a top, cradle me in your arms like a newborn. When confusion abounds, be my compass. When I am caught up in a hurricane of activity, draw me into the eye, so I may find peace amidst the chaos. For I would so love to skip with you along life's byways. Amen.

Prayers

Offer Personal Prayers and Thanksgiving.
Choose Collects from Parts Two, Three, or Four, as desired.

THE FATHER'S WOMB

The Word of the Father came from His womb and put on a body
in another womb.
She proceeded from one womb to another womb.
And chaste wombs are filled with Her.
Blessed is He who has resided in us.

ST. EPHREM THE SYRIAN'S *HYMNS OF RESURRECTION 1.7*

SONG OF PETER'S MOTHER-IN-LAW, MATTHEW 8: 14–15

What a dream!
I saw a light
as bright as the sun,
as warm as the sea.
I want to get up.
I've got work to do!
I want to get out.
I've got news to tell.
Jesus, the Lord, came right to my house!
The Son of God gives life to the dead.
The Holy Spirit herself comes to heal and cheer
from the tip of the toes to the top of the head!
Glory be, what a gift!
There's new life flowing deep inside of me.

CANA'S MAGNIFICENCE

Let Cana thank you because you brightened her wedding banquet.
The bridegroom's crown exalted you because you exalted it.
The bride's crown belonged to your victory.
Allegories are expounded and drawn in her mirror because you depicted your church in the bride.
In her companions, your guests are figured.
And in her magnificence, you depicted your coming.

St. Ephrem the Syrian's *Hymns of Virginity 33.1*

Closing

All things are ripened by warmth just as all things are sanctified by the Spirit, O visible type.

St. Ephrem the Syrian's *Hymns of Faith 74.9*

Evening Prayer

Greeting

I was glad when they said to me, "Let's go Home to Mother's House."

LOVE GOD, YOUR NEIGHBOR, AND YOURSELF

You shall love the Lord your God with all your heart, and with all your soul, and with all your strength, and with all your mind; and your neighbor as yourself.

Luke 10:27

COLLECT FOR EVENING

Divine Darkness, you separated the light from the darkness and pronounced both of them good. Our days and nights and twilight times are in your hands. Draw us close to you as evening approaches, so whether we wake or sleep or work or play, we rest wholly in you. For we pray in the name of the One who neither slumbers, nor sleeps, yet rested on the seventh day. Amen.

Prayers

Offer Personal Prayers and Thanksgiving.
Choose Collects from Parts Two, Three, or Four, as desired.

SONG OF LIGHT

Joyful Light,
Pure and bright,
Streaming from heaven's Loving God,
Jesus, the Anointed,

Holy, blessed Healing One,
As we light this vesper candle in Your Name,
We give thankful praises to you,
Loving God, Parent, Child, and Great Holy Spirit,
Especially to you, our Brother,
Child of God, Bearer of Life and Light,
Down through all generations.

Glory to you, God the Father and God the Mother,
Glory to you, Jesus Christ our Brother,
Glory to you, Great Holy Spirit. Amen.

RUTH, RUTH 3, AND TAMAR, GENESIS 38

Chaste women were chasing after men because of you:
Tamar desired a man who was widowed, and
Ruth loved a man who was old.
Also Rahab, who captivated men was captured by you.

Tamar went out in darkness and stole Light, and
she went out in uncleanness and stole the Holy One, and
she went out in nudity and stole for you, O Precious One,
who brings forth pure ones from promiscuous ones.

Satan saw her and was afraid and ran to obstruct her.
He reminded her of the punishment, yet she did not fear,
of stoning and the sword, yet she was not afraid.
He who teaches adultery was hindering adultery to hinder your birth.

For Tamar's adultery was holy for your sake.
She was thirsty for you, Pure Fountain.
Judah cheated her from drinking you.
The thirsty spring stole a drink of you, the Fount.

She was a widow for your sake.
She was desiring you and was even a prostitute for your sake.
She was longing for you, she watched and was sanctified.
She loved you.

Ruth is proclaimed who sought your riches instead of Moab.
Tamar rejoiced that her Lord, whom her very name proclaimed,
came, instead of the son of her bitterness.
Even her name was calling you to come to her (Ta "Come," Mar "Lord").

Honorable women became contemptible for you who make all modest.
She stole among the highways you who prepare the way to the house
of the kingdom.

Because she stole life, the sword was unable to kill her.

Ruth fell down in the threshing floor for a man for your sake.
Her love made her bold for your sake who teaches persistence
to all penitents.
Her ears despised all the voices for the sake of your voice.

The throbbing coal went up and fell down in Boaz's bed.
She saw the High Priest who was hidden in his loins:
She was fire for his incense.
She ran and was a heifer for Boaz.
She would bring forth you, the fatted calf.

She went begging for her love of you.
She gathered straw.
You paid her quickly the reward of her wretchedness.
She reaped the Root of kings instead of ears of corn and
the Sheaf of Life that descended from her instead of straw.

ST. EPHREM THE SYRIAN'S *HYMNS OF NATIVITY 9.7–16*

SONG OF THE STAR OF THE EAST

My being glorifies the Creator
with each cycle, each flicker of light, with each and every glow in the
night sky.
I am the Star of the East, the one who guided the magi and the sheep
with their shepherds to the stable where the Christ-child was born.

Along with the moon, my sister stars and I adorn the night sky. As we course through the sky, we serve as nocturnal signposts for navigators who cross the land or sea or sky.

During your span on Mother Earth, look to me. For by the ray of my sparkling light, I will guide you into the presence of the Divine Light, where you will sing with me,

"Glory be to the Luminous Three."

Closing

May the Darkness that revitalizes my soul attune me to the Harmony of Creation.

SECOND DAY, DAY OF THE MOON: DARKNESS AND HIDDEN-NESS

Morning Prayer

Greeting

The Mother of the saints rejoices and is glad.

Macarian Homily 27

WORDS OF COMFORT

For if John the Baptizer who was great called out, "I am not worthy to unfasten the straps of your sandals, O Lord," then like the fearful woman, I must take refuge in the shadow of your garment, that I might be loosened from fear.

And like that woman who was afraid and was comforted because she was healed, heal my awful trepidation, and I will be comforted by you.

Let me pass from your garment to your body, so I may speak of your body according to my strength.

St. Ephrem the Syrian's *Hymns of Faith 10.5–6*

COLLECT FOR MORNING

Morning Star, as the sun moves through the heavens, night becomes day. As the Spirit moves through the world, the dusks and dawns of life become holy ground. May I feel the sparkle of your radiance so deeply within that I am able to live fully into this day. Let my spirit play in your presence, regardless of what transpires. For I pray in the name of the Sacred Three. Amen.

Prayers

Offer Personal Prayers and Thanksgiving.
Choose Collects from Parts Two, Three, or Four, as desired.

HIDE AND SEEK WITH JESUS

If anyone seeks your hidden nature, lo, it is in heaven in the great
Womb of Divinity.
And if anyone seeks your revealed body, lo, it rests and looks out
from Mary's small womb.

St. Ephrem the Syrian's *Hymns of Nativity 13.7*

SONG OF THE BEAR CAVE

I am the cave for the hibernating
Bear, a sanctuary for rest
And birth and rebirth.

Remember the labor pains,
The strain, the push,
The cry of the newly born.
Remember the *joy!*

SONG OF THE FACES OF GOD

I am a crystal jug filled with Living Water.
I am a sponge ever squeezing out water to wipe the surfaces of life clean,
Soaking up, squeezing out,
Life-giving, Living Water.
I am the metamorphosis that transforms your life.
I was at the beginning
And I will be forever And Beyond . . .

Glory to you who fills,
Glory to you who squeezes,
Glory to you who transforms.

Closing

May the Light who lightens my life today illumine all of my tomorrows!

Midday Prayer

Greeting

Delight of my heart, rest in my peace; nestle into my presence.

JUSTICE

But let justice roll down like waters, and righteousness like an ever-flowing stream.

AMOS 5:24

COLLECT FOR MIDDAY

Holy Mystery, you are the life force that courses through my soul. When my world is spinning like a top, cradle me in your arms like a newborn. When confusion abounds, be my compass. When I am caught up in a hurricane of activity, draw me into the eye, so I may find peace amidst the chaos. For I would so love to skip with you along life's byways. Amen.

Prayers

Offer Personal Prayers and Thanksgiving.
Choose Collects from Parts Two, Three, or Four, as desired.

SONG OF THE ENDANGERED

Gracious Creator,
Through the millennia you scattered many wonderful creatures throughout this world we share.
Each one contributes to the rhythm of life and comes and goes in due course.
Now the continued existence of whole species is threatened.
We humans are growing like weeds and spreading like wildfire, but without the benefits they bring to their environment.
Weeds provide beauty and healing through their flowers.
Wildfires help forests sustain themselves and open up the woods to new life.
Too often, we simply destroy.
The lives of creatures great and small are endangered: bears, beetles, and butterflies, jaguars, Bengal tigers, whales, and the red cockaded woodpecker, Adélie penguins, and polar bears.
Many kinds of plants, like wild orchids, are being lost simply because humans like to play God instead of appreciating the magnanimous gift of variety you have given us.
Whole ecosystems, like wetlands and prairies, rainforests and glaciers, are disappearing.
Yes, Great Spirit, we have lost the sense of the balance it takes to live in harmony with creation.
We lift up the people of the world and pray for an awakening before it's too late.
We ask for your guidance in channeling our energies into creative, rather than destructive, directions, for the sake of your precious creation.

Glory to you who creates,
Glory to you who sustains,
Glory to you who awakens.

A GREAT WONDER

It is a great wonder that he did not proceed gradually from that height to descend and come to littleness.
He flew from the Womb of Divinity to the womb of humanity.
I give thanks for your first birth, which was hidden and concealed from all creation.
I also give thanks for your second birth, which was revealed and younger than all creation.
Yet they are in your hands.

I give thanks for the births of the Only-Begotten, one above and one below, one the stranger that is strange to all, and one the kinsman that is entirely connected to humanity.

St. Ephrem the Syrian's *Hymns of Nativity 27.15, 19–20*

Closing

All things are ripened by warmth just as all things are sanctified by the Spirit, O visible type.

St. Ephrem the Syrian's *Hymns of Faith 74.9*

Evening Prayer

Greeting

I was glad when they said to me, "Let's go Home to Mother's House."

FOR LOVE'S SAKE

This prayer is intended to be prayed in parts, with one person or group praying the lines in regular type, and the other person or group praying the lines in boldface. Those who are praying alone may wish to pray one line silently and the other aloud.

Into your heart, O God, we commend those who live on the edge, whether by choice or through no fault of their own.

Teach us to love, O Lover of life.

Into your rest, O God, we commend those who live in a whirlwind of activity.

Teach us to love, O Lover of life.

Into your presence, O God, we commend those we hurt, whether carelessly, unintentionally, or deliberately.

Teach us to love, O Lover of life.

Into your hands, O God, we commend our loved ones and the strangers in our midst.

Teach us to love, O Lover of life.

Into your depths, O God, we commend our inner lives and our outer journeys.

Teach us to love, O Lover of life.

COLLECT FOR EVENING

Divine Darkness, you separated the light from the darkness and pronounced both of them good. Our days and nights and twilight times are in your hands. Draw us close to you as evening approaches, so whether we wake or sleep or work or play, we rest wholly in you. For we pray in the name of the One who neither slumbers, nor sleeps, yet rested on the seventh day. Amen.

Prayers

Offer Personal Prayers and Thanksgiving.
Choose Collects from Parts Two, Three, or Four, as desired.

SONG OF ARIANRHOD

I am the Moon Goddess of Wales.
I am like a silver wheel, the keeper of the cycles of life,
of time here on Earth and in Heaven itself.
From my celestial palace in the night sky,
I oversee the souls waiting to be born into this world.
I am with you in times of darkness and anguish, and in times of light.
Watch my wheel spin in the moonlight. It turns for you and for your future.

Glory to you who keeps,
Glory to you who oversees,
Glory to you who spins.

FULL MOON

Sing aloud to God our strength;
Raise a song, sound the tambourine, the sweet lyre with the harp.
Blow the trumpet at the new moon, at the full moon, on our festal day.
PSALM 81:1–3

SONG OF DARK PLACES AND SECRET SPACES

You, O God, are the Rock of our Creation.
Stalagmites rise up to meet you, while stalactites inch down to greet you.
Caves seep with your mysterious splendor.
Caverns reek of your ineffable majesty.
We remember the divine breath deftly moving among ions,
the touch of holy hands playing in the mud.
We thrill to the memory of God's still small voice in our midst.
You, O God, are the Rock of our Salvation.

Glory to you, O Mystery,
Glory to you, O Breath,
Glory to you, O Voice.

AN ALTERNATIVE LORD'S PRAYER

Eternal Spirit,
Life-Giver, Pain-Bearer, Love-Maker
Source of all that is and all that shall be,
Father and Mother of us all,

Loving God, in whom is heaven:
The hallowing of your name echo through the universe!
The way of your justice be followed by the people of the world!
Your heavenly will be done by all created beings!
Your commonwealth of peace and freedom sustain our hope, and
come on earth!
With the bread we need for today, feed us.
In the hurts we absorb from one another, forgive us.
In times of temptation and test, strengthen us.
From trials too severe to endure, spare us.
From the grip of all that is evil, free us.
For you reign in the glory of the power that is love,
now and for ever. Amen.

JIM COTTER

Closing

May the Darkness that revitalizes my soul attune me to the Harmony of Creation.

THIRD DAY, DAY OF TIW: PEACE

Morning Prayer

Greeting

The Mother of the saints rejoices and is glad.

MACARIAN HOMILY 27

WALK HUMBLY

He has told you, O mortal, what is good; and what does the Lord require of you, but to do justice, and to love kindness, and to walk humbly with your God?

MICAH 6:8

COLLECT FOR MORNING

Morning Star, as the sun moves through the heavens, night becomes day. As the Spirit moves through the world, the dusks and dawns of life become holy ground. May I feel the sparkle of your radiance so deeply within that I am able to live fully into this day. Let my spirit play in your presence, regardless of what transpires. For I pray in the name of the Sacred Three. Amen.

Prayers

Offer Personal Prayers and Thanksgiving.
Choose Collects from Parts Two, Three, or Four, as desired.

WINGS OF THE SPIRIT

Like the wings of doves over their chicks with the chicks' beaks turned towards their own beaks, so also are the wings of the Spirit over my heart.

My heart is refreshed and leaps for joy, like the baby who leapt for joy in his mother's womb.

Odes of Solomon 28:1–2

SONG OF THE WHITE BUFFALO CALF WOMAN

(The White Buffalo Calf Woman brought the sacred pipe—commonly called "peace pipe"—to the Lakota.)

Bring the children to me;
Tell them to be at ease.
Bring the children to me;
We will talk not war but peace.
Bring the children to me,
Worn and wounded from the war;
Bring the children to me,
Those bound and burned and scarred.

Bring the children to me;
They no longer have to roam.
Bring the children to me;
We will talk instead of home.
Bring the children to me
To heal war's dark disease.
Bring the children to me
To smoke the pipe of peace.

ANNA, PROPHETESS AND EVANGELIST, LUKE 2:36–38

Blessed are you, fair old Anna, for the silent Infant made you a prophetess, for his hidden silence thundered in your mind so that he might sing of his exploits in you.
He interpreted his actions when young through you, but he will complete them himself when he matures.
The Infant who is the Lord of all mouths, when silent, sang in every language.

Blessed are you, old woman, treasure of perception, for this ancient Infant met you.
Therefore, the Infant, who came to betroth souls, betrothed you, old woman, first of all.
He made you the first of all of them, and by your old age, he assigned youth its place.
He polished a mirror and set it up for children to learn dignity.

St. Ephrem the Syrian's *Hymns of Virginity 25.15–16*

Closing

May the Light who lightens my life today illumine all of my tomorrows!

Midday Prayer

Greeting

Delight of my heart, rest in my peace; nestle into my presence.

LOVE GOD, YOUR NEIGHBOR, AND YOURSELF

You shall love the Lord your God with all your heart, and with all your soul, and with all your strength, and with all your mind, and your neighbor as yourself.

Luke 10:27

COLLECT FOR MIDDAY

Holy Mystery, you are the life force that courses through my soul. When my world is spinning like a top, cradle me in your arms like a newborn. When confusion abounds, be my compass. When I am caught up in a hurricane of activity, draw me into the eye, so I may find peace amidst the chaos. For I would so love to skip with you along life's byways. Amen.

Prayers

Offer Personal Prayers and Thanksgiving.
Choose Collects from Parts Two, Three, or Four, as desired.

ANNA, PROPHETESS AND EVANGELIST, LUKE 2:36–38

Anna embraced Him;
she put her mouth on His lips, and
the Spirit rested on her lips as it did on Isaiah's,
whose mouth was quiet until a coal approached his lips and opened his mouth.

St. Ephrem the Syrian's *Hymns of Nativity 6.13*

MARY AS PRIEST AND PROPHET, LUKE 2:22–40

The son comes to the servant, not so the son may be offered up to God by the servant,

But through the son the servant will offer the priesthood and prophecy that were commended to him. . . . When therefore both priesthood and prophecy saw their Lord, they commingled in each other. And they were poured into that vessel (Jesus) that ultimately provides both of them,

that vessel that contains priesthood, monarchy, and prophecy. That infant then who was swaddled in swaddling clothes clothed himself in priesthood because of his goodness and in prophecy because of his greatness. For Simeon was clothed in them, and he gave him to the one who had swaddled him in swaddling clothes. When Simeon gave him to his mother, he gave her with him priesthood, and when he prophesied to her concerning him this, "He is set for the fall and for rising," he gave her with him prophecy also.

St. Ephrem the Syrian's *Sermons of our Lord 53*

SONG OF EXPANSES

In the beginning God created chronos, kairos, time,
And there were many mornings and evenings as a great expanse of time passed.
At the mid-point God created space, the cosmos, the universe,
And there were many dawns and dusks as a great expanse of the universe passed.
Toward the end God creates everything out there and all that's in here,
And there will be many noontimes and midnights as a great expanse of life passes.

Glory to you who begins;
Glory to you who sustains;
Glory to you who completes.

Closing

All things are ripened by warmth just as all things are sanctified by the Spirit, O visible type.

St. Ephrem the Syrian's *Hymns of Faith 74.9*

Evening Prayer

Greeting

I was glad when they said to me, "Let's go Home to Mother's House."

LOVE GOD, YOUR NEIGHBOR, AND YOURSELF

You shall love the Lord your God with all your heart, and with all your soul, and with all your strength, and with all your mind, and your neighbor as yourself.

LUKE 10:27

COLLECT FOR EVENING

Divine Darkness, you separated the light from the darkness and pronounced both of them good. Our days and nights and twilight times are in your hands. Draw us close to you as evening approaches, so whether we wake or sleep or work or play, we rest wholly in you. For we pray in the name of the One who neither slumbers, nor sleeps, yet rested on the seventh day. Amen.

Prayers

Offer Personal Prayers and Thanksgiving.
Choose Collects from Parts Two, Three, or Four, as desired.

SONG OF ANNA

Lo, the ways of the Divine are rare.
My soul soared when I saw Mary strolling up to the temple with her new baby in her arms.
When the baby's eyes met mine, I felt as radiant as a young bride.
Or like Moses, after he went up on Mount Sinai and beheld you, O Holy One, face to face.
What a God we have!
One who sends us the Holiness of the Ages in a tiny baby, and gives new life to an old woman who's facing death.
Praise to you, Holy Comforter.
For you've used the ordinary ways of women to do something extraordinary.
My spirit leapt within me when I saw Jesus' dear little face.
What joy!
Finally to see the new baby after a long and difficult labor.
I felt like an eagle ready to take off, to spread the word!
I say it now for all generations:
Mary's son is the Messiah, the Christ, God's Anointed One!
The one we've been waiting for, for so long.
Spread the word! The Spirit of God is upon us.

SONG OF SHE-WHO-BEHOLDS-THE-BEAUTY-OF-HER-LORD

I sit, stand, and breathe in the beauty of my Lord.
And God's beauty transforms me.
I am the golden base on which the candle stands.

I am the bronze mirror reflecting the essence of my God.
I am the instrument that echoes the divine melody—lustrous and serene.
I behold holy beauty.
I live a life of beauty.
Look with me so you, too, may behold the beauty of the Divine all around you.

Glory to you who inspires,
Glory to you who transforms,
Glory to you who sings.

WITHOUT LIMIT

God saw that we worshipped created things.
He put on a created body so that he might trap us by our habit.
Behold by this formed one the Former restored us, and by this creation our Creator revived us. He did not force us.
Blessed is he who came in that which is ours and mixed us in that which is his.
Blessed is he who became small without limit so that we might become great without limit.

St. Ephrem the Syrian's *Hymns of Nativity 21.12, refrain*

AN ALTERNATIVE LORD'S PRAYER

Eternal Spirit,
Life-Giver, Pain-Bearer, Love-Maker
Source of all that is and all that shall be,
Father and Mother of us all,
Loving God, in whom is heaven:
The hallowing of your name echo through the universe!
The way of your justice be followed by the people of the world!
Your heavenly will be done by all created beings!
Your commonwealth of peace and freedom sustain our hope, and come on earth!
With the bread we need for today, feed us.
In the hurts we absorb from one another, forgive us.
In times of temptation and test, strengthen us.
From trials too severe to endure, spare us.
From the grip of all that is evil, free us.
For you reign in the glory of the power that is love,
now and for ever. Amen.

Jim Cotter

Closing

May the Darkness that revitalizes my soul attune me to the Harmony of Creation.

FOURTH DAY, DAY OF WODIN: WISDOM

Morning Prayer

Greeting

The Mother of the saints rejoices and is glad.
MACARIAN HOMILY 27

WORDS OF COMFORT

For if John the Baptizer who was great called out, "I am not worthy to unfasten the straps of Your sandals, O Lord," then like the fearful woman, I must take refuge in the shadow of your garment, that I might be loosened from fear.
And like that woman who was afraid and was comforted because she was healed, heal my awful trepidation, and I will be comforted by you.
Let me pass from your garment to your body, so I may speak of your body according to my strength.
ST. EPHREM THE SYRIAN'S *HYMNS OF FAITH 10.5–6*

COLLECT FOR MORNING

Morning Star, as the sun moves through the heavens, night becomes day. As the Spirit moves through the world, the dusks and dawns of life become holy ground. May I feel the sparkle of your radiance so deeply within that I am able to live fully into this day. Let my spirit play in your presence, regardless of what transpires. For I pray in the name of the Sacred Three. Amen.

Prayers

Offer Personal Prayers and Thanksgiving.
Choose Collects from Parts Two, Three, or Four, as desired.

DIVINITY AS A NURSING MOTHER

The Divinity is attentive to us like a nursing mother with a child,
who keeps his feeding schedule, who knows when he will be weaned,
and how long he will grow with milk, and how long he will be nourished with bread.

And She weighs him and gives him more food according to the state of his development.

St. Ephrem the Syrian's *Hymns of the Church 25.18*

LOVE OF WISDOM

Wisdom is radiant and unfading, and she is easily discerned by those who love her, and is found by those who seek her.
She hastens to make herself known to those who desire her.
One who rises early to seek her will have no difficulty, for she will be found sitting at the gate.
To fix one's thoughts on her is perfect understanding, and one who is vigilant on her account will soon be free from care, because she goes about seeking those worthy of her, and She graciously appears to them in their paths, and meets them in every thought.
The beginning of wisdom is the most sincere desire for instruction, and concern for instruction is love of her, and
love of her is the keeping of her laws, and giving heed to her laws is assurance of immortality, and immortality brings one near to God.

Wisdom of Solomon 6:12–19

Closing

May the Light who lightens my life today illumine all of my tomorrows!

Midday Prayer

Greeting

Delight of my heart, rest in my peace; nestle into my presence.

LOVE ONE ANOTHER

This is my commandment, that you love one another as I have loved you.

John 15:12

COLLECT FOR MIDDAY

Holy Mystery, you are the life force that courses through my soul. When my world is spinning like a top, cradle me in your arms like a newborn. When confusion abounds, be my compass. When I am caught up in a hurricane of activity, draw me into the eye, so I may find peace amidst the chaos. For I would so love to skip with you along life's byways. Amen.

Prayers

Offer Personal Prayers and Thanksgiving.
Choose Collects from Parts Two, Three, or Four, as desired.

WISDOM, THE FASHIONER OF ALL THINGS

May God grant me to speak with judgment, and to have thoughts worthy of what I have received; for he is the guide even of wisdom and the corrector of the wise.
For both we and our words are in his hand, as are all understanding and skill in crafts.
For it is he who gave me unerring knowledge of what exists,
to know the structure of the world and the activity of the elements;
the beginnings and end and middle of times,
the alternations of the solstices and the changes of the seasons,
the cycles of the year and the constellations of the stars,
the natures of animals and the tempers of wild animals,
the powers of spirits and the thoughts of human beings,
the varieties of plants and the virtues of roots;
I learned both what is secret and what is manifest,
For wisdom, the fashioner of all things, taught me.

WISDOM OF SOLOMON 7:15–22

SONG OF CHANGING WOMAN

(The One who presides over the changing roles in a woman's life, from a girl's coming of age and wedding, to becoming a mother and later an elder.)

Would you be wise? Then learn this from me,
The wisest always come dancing with me,
Through grassy plains; along the edge of the sea,
Down country roads, and up city streets.

Would you be wise? Then learn this from me,
The wisest always are playing with me,
Wearing a mask, an ingenious disguise,
Changing their hair, and painting their eyes.

Would you be wise? Then learn this from me,
The wisest always come flying with me,
Discovering the soul's Spirit Lands, crying in the night,
Keening with the Wild Geese and flying toward Life!

Would you be wise? Then learn this from me,
The wisest dance and play and fly with me,
Exploring the soul's Spirit Lands, calling in the night,
Singing with the Wild Geese—flying toward Love and Life!

THE MIND AS MOTHER

Oh my tongue! Stop and quiet the continuous stories of the cross, for my mind has suddenly conceived, and lo, labor pains afflict it.
It conceived these ideas among the last born, but they want to be the firstborn.

St. Ephrem the Syrian's *Songs of Nisibis 14.11*

Closing

All things are ripened by warmth just as all things are sanctified by the Spirit, O visible type.

St. Ephrem the Syrian's *Hymns of Faith 74.9*

Evening Prayer

Greeting

I was glad when they said to me, "Let's go Home to Mother's House."

WALK HUMBLY

He has told you, O mortal, what is good; and what does the Lord require of you, but to do justice, and to love kindness, and to walk humbly with your God?

Micah 6:8

COLLECT FOR EVENING

Divine Darkness, you separated the light from the darkness and pronounced both of them good. Our days and nights and twilight times are in your hands. Draw us close to you as evening approaches, so whether we wake or sleep or work or play, we rest wholly in you. For we pray in the name of the One who neither slumbers, nor sleeps, yet rested on the seventh day. Amen.

Prayers

Offer Personal Prayers and Thanksgiving.
Choose Collects from Parts Two, Three, or Four, as desired.

THE SAMARITAN WOMAN, JOHN 4:7–30, 39, AND TAMAR, GENESIS 38

Blessed are you, drawer of ordinary water, who turned out to be a drawer of living water. You found the treasure, another Fount, from whom a flood of mercies flows. The spring had dried up, but it broke through to you and gave you water. He had become poor, but he asked for a drink to enrich you. You left your pitcher, but you filled your thoughts from the Fount and gave living water to your people.

Blessed are you, woman, because you saw that your husbands were dead, and your reproaches were many. Other men were afraid to take you in marriage, lest they die like their companions. You made a contract with a pretended and bribed husband. He overcame your reproach, but he did not approach your body. The contract and the oaths that you made secretly he revealed to you, and you put your faith in him.

For she answered and spoke as a trained one, controversially, but chastely, "Our fathers worshipped on this mountain." Since the heads of her people were of the house of Abraham, she did not need to ask about her offenses, for her love was bound with the just. Since he revealed to her one thing, she thought he would teach her truth without strife.

She answered again, saying prudently, "Lord I see that you are a prophet." If, indeed, our Lord revealed her shame to her, it would be right for her to receive compassion in judgment like the sinful woman who sought forgiveness with her head bowed and also her mouth closed. But she was modest, yet her head was held high and her voice authoritative.

She said, "I have no husband," to tell him the truth and to test him in two ways: what she did have and what she did not now have—to see if he would be able to comprehend her secrets. Our Lord revealed both of them and amazed her, for she did have a husband, but she did not now have one. She was astonished and persuaded; she was amazed and believed; and she professed and worshipped him.

Therefore when she concealed her secret mystery and heard the saying about living water, she proved him with this sign, "If he reveals to me the existing marriage contract, then he is God." Our Lord revealed to her this secret of hers and gave her water, and she did not thirst for worldly water. She left the mortal man and did not seek his protection, for the Living One betrothed and took her as a wife.

She spoke fairly, and our Lord confirmed concerning that man that he was not her husband. But he revealed that he existed, and if he had been lascivious, Jesus would not have been able to conceal it completely because he was trusted and proclaimed by her. Therefore she to whom he said "he exists," witnesses that he was old or poor and lived under her protection as she lived under his.

Tamar trusted that the king whose symbol she stole would arise from Judah. Also this woman among the Samaritans expected that perhaps the Messiah would arise from her. Tamar's hope was not extinguished, this woman's expectation was not in vain, as from her, therefore, our Lord arose in this city, for he was revealed by her there.

Because she, in her desire, said, "The Messiah will come," he revealed to her with love, "I am he." She believed he was a prophet before; a little later she believed also that he was the Messiah. O Wise One, who appeared as a thirsty man, and a little later, was called a prophet, and then she understood he is the Messiah; she is a type of our humanity that he leads in every step.

St. Ephrem the Syrian's *Hymns of Virginity 22.2, 4, 6–8, 12–13, 20–21*

WISDOM, AN IMAGE OF GOD'S GOODNESS

> For wisdom is more mobile than any motion; because of her pureness she pervades and penetrates all things. For she is a breath of the power of God . . . For she is a reflection of eternal light, a spotless mirror of the working of God, and an image of his goodness.
>
> Wisdom of Solomon 7:24–26

Closing

May the Darkness that revitalizes my soul attune me to the Harmony of Creation.

FIFTH DAY, DAY OF THONAR: THUNDER AND SKY

Morning Prayer

Greeting

The Mother of the saints rejoices and is glad.

Macarian Homily 27

WALK HUMBLY

He has told you, O mortal, what is good; and what does the Lord require of you, but to do justice, and to love kindness, and to walk humbly with your God?

Micah 6:8

COLLECT FOR MORNING

Morning Star, as the sun moves through the heavens, night becomes day. As the Spirit moves through the world, the dusks and dawns of life become holy ground. May I feel the sparkle of your radiance so deeply within that I am able to live fully into this day. Let my spirit play in your presence, regardless of what transpires. For I pray in the name of the Sacred Three. Amen.

Prayers

Offer Personal Prayers and Thanksgiving.
Choose Collects from Parts Two, Three, or Four, as desired.

SONG OF SHE-WHO-BEATS-THE-RHYTHM

I am Time-in-Motion.
My body moves with every beat of the music.
I feel the pulses deep down in my soul.
The rhythm of the music seeps from my inner being out along my limbs
and into the hearts of my instruments—harp, drums, and sistra.
I am time moving—plucking, beating, pulsing.
Time moves through me,
like a dove soars through the sky,
like a fish swims in the sea,
like a camel gallumps through the sand.
Come! Join me in this holy movement to praise the Holy One.

THE CANAANITE WOMAN, MATTHEW 15:21–28

You, too, daughter of Canaan, conquered the Unconquerable One by boldness for that justice. The Just One set a boundary for the land of the Gentiles that the Gospel might not cross over. Blessed are you who broke through the fence fearlessly. The Lord of boundaries extolled you for the strength of your faith. He healed your daughter inside your house from afar.

ST. EPHREM THE SYRIAN'S *HYMNS OF VIRGINITY 26.9*

SONG OF THUNDER

Thunder Beings are we, some gentle rumbles, some all-out roars.
We awoke to the big bang of the Divine Voice calling creation
into being,
and we responded to the rich, warm sound.
From the dawn of time we've vibrated to the beat of the Maker of
the cosmos,
at the watering of Mother Earth, in the symphony of creation.
Our voices have sounded throughout the ages.
We may sing joyfully like a man in a shower or softly like a baby
in a bath
or growl fearfully like a mother bear whose cubs are threatened.
Like tympani, we boom out for all to hear,
Come join in the drama. Dance with the Harmony of Creation.
Live with the Lover of Life.

Closing

May the Light who lightens my life today illumine all of my tomorrows!

Midday Prayer

Greeting

Delight of my heart, rest in my peace; nestle into my presence.

LOVE ONE ANOTHER

This is my commandment, that you love one another as I have loved you.
JOHN 15:12

COLLECT FOR MIDDAY

Holy Mystery, you are the life force that courses through my soul. When my world is spinning like a top, cradle me in your arms like a newborn. When confusion abounds, be my compass. When I am caught up in a hurricane of activity, draw me into the eye, so I may find peace amidst the chaos. For I would so love to skip with you along life's byways. Amen.

Prayers

Offer Personal Prayers and Thanksgiving.
Choose Collects from Parts Two, Three, or Four, as desired.

SECRET PLACE OF THUNDER

I hear a voice I had not known: I relieved your shoulder of the burden; your hands were freed from the basket. In distress you called, and I rescued you; I answered you in the secret place of thunder.
PSALM 81:5B–7A

SONG OF THE EXTINCT

Pantokrator, Maker of Life,
We sigh in the memory of the mighty and the meek, those who traversed the Earth long ago—dinosaurs, mammoths, and dodo birds—and also the plants, birds, and insects that have become extinct in our own life times.
So many, like the ivory billed woodpecker and laysan rail, are now known only to specialists.
We lament the trees and plants that no longer grace the face of Mother Earth.
What joy it would be to see Hawaii's plants called nehe and haha.

We mourn the loss of entire groups of peoples, languages, and their religious and cultural rituals.
All came into being and took their place in the world, each according to their own kinds and purposes.
Some live on in their bones and artifacts in the fossil and archaeological records.
With the extinction of their kinds, some left their marks, while others vanished without a trace.
We praise you for gathering their energies back into the Cosmic All of Divinity.

JESUS, FELLOW-CREATURE TO REPTILES AND ANIMALS

Who would not be astonished that if even His Son is a servant,
then the womb of His Parent made Him a fellow-creature to everything?
And He was indeed more glorious in the birth from Mary that made Him a true brother to humanity,
than from the Womb that made Him a fellow-creature of all—even reptiles and animals.

ST. EPHREM THE SYRIAN'S *HYMNS OF FAITH 62.10*

Closing

All things are ripened by warmth just as all things are sanctified by the Spirit, O visible type.

ST. EPHREM THE SYRIAN'S *HYMNS OF FAITH 74.9*

Evening Prayer

Greeting

I was glad when they said to me, "Let's go Home to Mother's House."

JUSTICE

But let justice roll down like waters, and righteousness like an ever-flowing stream.

AMOS 5:24

COLLECT FOR EVENING

Divine Darkness, you separated the light from the darkness and pronounced both of them good. Our days and nights and twilight times are in your hands. Draw us close to you as evening approaches, so whether we wake or sleep or work or play, we rest wholly in you. For we pray in the name of the One who neither slumbers, nor sleeps, yet rested on the seventh day. Amen.

Prayers

Offer Personal Prayers and Thanksgiving.
Choose Collects from Parts Two, Three, or Four, as desired.

SONG FOR EARTH DAY: PELE SPEAKS

Pele, Goddess of Volcanoes, fiery-eyed
Fiery hair streaming,
Hurling semi-molten boulders
Through the air,
Spouting obsidian
Into the darkening night.
What is the source of your anger?
At whom do you fling your invectives?
Tell me, Goddess,
Of your wounds,
Of your irritants,
Your stresses.

"I am the Goddess Pele.
I am the fiery-tressed.
I am woman and
I am angry! No . . . I . . . am . . . DISTRESSED!

Mother Earth is overstressed
Father Sky is lowering
Ocean waters polluted
Population growing.

Winds from the four directions
Spread acid rain and forest fire,
Nitrogen and sulfur-dioxide—
Atmospheric conditions: dire.

Studies of circumpolar currents
Show ozone depletion.
Life is in the balance
Possibly nearing completion.

Fiery core of earth,
Convective currents flowing,
Slip zones, trench faults straining
Sudden shifts and glowing

Geysers of lava
Spewing forth in the night
Cower, human, cringe
Crouch down in fright.

Watch my pyrotechnics,
Stand in awe or flee—
In your hurried negotiations,
Why don't you learn to be?"

FIRE AND SPIRIT

Lo, fire and Spirit in the womb of her who brought you forth.
Lo, fire and Spirit in the river in which you were baptized,
fire and Spirit in our baptism,
fire and the Holy Spirit in the bread and cup.

St. Ephrem the Syrian's *Hymns of Faith 10.17*

EVERY TEAR FROM THEIR EYES

For this reason they are before the throne of God,
And worship him, day and night within the temple,
And the one who is seated on the throne will shelter them.
They will hunger no more, and thirst no more;
The sun will not strike them, nor any scorching heat;
For the Lamb at the center of the throne will be their shepherd,
And he will guide them to springs of the water of life,
And God will wipe away every tear from their eyes.

Revelation 7:15–17

AN ALTERNATIVE LORD'S PRAYER

Eternal Spirit,
Life-Giver, Pain-Bearer, Love-Maker
Source of all that is and all that shall be,
Father and Mother of us all,
Loving God, in whom is heaven:
The hallowing of your name echo through the universe!
The way of your justice be followed by the people of the world!
Your heavenly will be done by all created beings!
Your commonwealth of peace and freedom sustain our hope and come on earth!
With the bread we need for today, feed us.
In the hurts we absorb from one another, forgive us.
In times of temptation and test, strengthen us.

From trials too severe to endure, spare us.
From the grip of all that is evil, free us.
For you reign in the glory of the power that is love,
now and for ever. Amen.
JIM COTTER

Closing

May the Darkness that revitalizes my soul attune me to the Harmony of Creation.

SIXTH DAY, DAY OF FREYA: LOVE

Morning Prayer

Greeting

The Mother of the saints rejoices and is glad.
MACARIAN HOMILY 27

WORDS OF COMFORT

For if John the Baptizer who was great called out, "I am not worthy to unfasten the straps of your sandals, O Lord," then like the fearful woman, I must take refuge in the shadow of your garment, that I might be loosened from fear. And like that woman who was afraid and was comforted because she was healed, heal my awful trepidation, and I will be comforted by you. Let me pass from your garment to your body, so I may speak of your body according to my strength.
ST. EPHREM THE SYRIAN'S *HYMNS OF FAITH 10.5–6*

COLLECT FOR MORNING

Morning Star, as the sun moves through the heavens, night becomes day. As the Spirit moves through the world, the dusks and dawns of life become holy ground. May I feel the sparkle of your radiance so deeply within that I am able to live fully into this day. Let my spirit play in your presence, regardless of what transpires. For I pray in the name of the Sacred Three. Amen.

Prayers

Offer Personal Prayers and Thanksgiving.
Choose Collects from Parts Two, Three, or Four, as desired.

SONG OF FREYA

I am the Goddess of Love.
My love is great, like a sow's for her piglets, all thirteen of them.
I have milk aplenty for all to drink.
Come fill your cup as I fill your soul and body with my abundance.
In days of yore,
my festival was marked by eating fish and making love in the countryside.
My milk gives strength to your frame.
My fish gives power to your head.
My love gives joy to your heart.
Take care, beware of how you treat yourself.
Take care, be fair in how you share my love.

MARY, JOHN, AND THE SEERS, JOHN 19:25B–27

Blessed are you, O woman, for your Lord and your son entrusted and gave you to one who is formed in his image. The son of your womb did not wrong your love; he entrusted and gave you to the son of his womb. You embraced him upon your breast when he was small, and he also embraced that one upon his breast. When he was crucified, he paid back the debt of his upbringing.

Since the Crucified One repaid debts, yours also was repaid by him. He sucked visible milk from your breast, and John sucked hidden mysteries from his breast. Confidently he approached your breast; confidently John approached and lay upon his breast. Since you entreated him, he gave you his harp to comfort you.

For they saw you, Lord, in themselves . . . while they were observing each other. Your mother saw you in your disciple; and he saw you in your mother. O, the seers, who see you, Lord, in each other at every moment as in a mirror, are a type that we also might see you, our Savior, in each other

St. Ephrem the Syrian's *Hymns of Virginity 25.2–3, 9*

Closing

May the Light who lightens my life today illumine all of my tomorrows!

Midday Prayer

Greeting

Delight of my heart, rest in my peace; nestle into my presence.

LOVE ONE ANOTHER

This is my commandment, that you love one another as I have loved you.
JOHN 15:12

COLLECT FOR MIDDAY

Holy Mystery, you are the life force that courses through my soul. When my world is spinning like a top, cradle me in your arms like a newborn. When confusion abounds, be my compass. When I am caught up in a hurricane of activity, draw me into the eye, so I may find peace amidst the chaos. For I would so love to skip with you along life's byways. Amen.

Prayers

Offer Personal Prayers and Thanksgiving.
Choose Collects from Parts Two, Three, or Four, as desired.

LOVE, STRONG AS DEATH

Set me as a seal upon your heart, as a seal upon your arm; for love is strong as death, passion fierce as the grave. Its flashes are flashes of fire, a raging flame. Many waters cannot quench love, neither can floods drown it. If one offered for love all the wealth of one's house, it would be utterly scorned.
SONG OF SOLOMON 8:6–7

FOR LOVE'S SAKE

This prayer is intended to be prayed in parts, with one person or group praying the lines in regular type, and the other person or group praying the lines in boldface. Those who are praying alone may wish to pray one line silently and the other aloud.

Into your heart, O God, we commend those who live on the edge, whether by choice or through no fault of their own.
Teach us to love, O Lover of life.
Into your rest, O God, we commend those who live in a whirlwind of activity.
Teach us to love, O Lover of life.
Into your presence, O God, we commend those we hurt, whether carelessly, unintentionally, or deliberately.
Teach us to love, O Lover of life.
Into your hands, O God, we commend our loved ones and the strangers in our midst.
Teach us to love, O Lover of life.
Into your depths, O God, we commend our inner lives and our outer journeys.
Teach us to love, O Lover of life.

A DAUGHTER TO MARY, LUKE 10:39

Blessed are you if you will be a daughter to Mary whose eye despised all persons. She turned her face away from everything and gazed on one beauty alone. Blessed is her love that was intoxicated, not sober, so that she sat at his feet to gaze at him. Let yourself also imagine the Messiah in your heart, and love him in your mind.

St. Ephrem the Syrian's *Hymns of Virginity 24.7*

Closing

All things are ripened by warmth just as all things are sanctified by the Spirit, O visible type.

St. Ephrem the Syrian's *Hymns of Faith 74.9*

Evening Prayer

Greeting

I was glad when they said to me, "Let's go Home to Mother's House."

WALK HUMBLY

He has told you, O mortal, what is good; and what does the Lord require of you, but to do justice, and to love kindness, and to walk humbly with your God?

Micah 6:8

COLLECT FOR EVENING

Divine Darkness, you separated the light from the darkness and pronounced both of them good. Our days and nights and twilight times are in your hands. Draw us close to you as evening approaches, so whether we wake or sleep or work or play, we rest wholly in you. For we pray in the name of the One who neither slumbers, nor sleeps, yet rested on the seventh day. Amen.

Prayers

Offer Personal Prayers and Thanksgiving.
Choose Collects from Parts Two, Three, or Four, as desired.

SONG OF LILITH

I was the first woman, created before Eve.
Too energetic was I to be confined to Adam's expectations.
Too determined was I to be contained within the walls of Eden.

I was the first woman, created as wild as the garden itself.
Too independent was I to be contented with propriety.
Too adventurous was I to be concerned with security.

So out of the garden I skipped.
Then out of the story I slipped.
Sing no dirges for me.
Pity me not.

I was the first woman, confident and carefree,
Within Eden's walls and beyond.
Co-creator of all I see.

With the joy of creating comes Wisdom.
Like all life, we need both darkness and light to thrive.
Restfully re-create our world with me.
Enjoy the beauty of all you see.

HANNAH'S OFFERING, 1 SAMUEL 2:1–10

O Lord, my mind is sterile of giving birth to new things. Give fruit and give birth to my mind as you gave to Hannah, so that the utterance of the child that will come forth from my mouth may be offered to you as was the son of that sterile woman.

St. Ephrem the Syrian's *Hymns of the Church 30.1*

AN ALTERNATIVE LORD'S PRAYER

Eternal Spirit,
Life-Giver, Pain-Bearer, Love-Maker
Source of all that is and all that shall be,
Father and Mother of us all,
Loving God, in whom is heaven:
The hallowing of your name echo through the universe!
The way of your justice be followed by the people of the world!
Your heavenly will be done by all created beings!
Your commonwealth of peace and freedom sustain our hope, and come on earth!
With the bread we need for today, feed us.
In the hurts we absorb from one another, forgive us.
In times of temptation and test, strengthen us.
From trials too severe to endure, spare us.
From the grip of all that is evil, free us.
For you reign in the glory of the power that is love,
now and for ever. Amen.

Jim Cotter

Closing

May the Darkness that revitalizes my soul attune me to the Harmony of Creation.

SEVENTH DAY, DAY OF SATURN: SOWING SEED

Morning Prayer

Greeting

The Mother of the saints rejoices and is glad.
MACARIAN HOMILY 27

AL-'ASMA' AL-HUSNA, "THE BEAUTIFUL NAMES"

Holy One of One-Hundred Beautiful Names,
three of which are Compassion, Love, and Mercy,
I acknowledge my offenses against you and your creation.
In my attempts to be holy, too often I have listened to others
instead of trusting my own God-given instincts.
I have accepted distorted images of women for so long
that I no longer recognize the godly goodness of my own voice.
I have tarnished the unique God-shaped image that you so tenderly created inside
each one of us, female and male.
I confess the times I have not loved you, Creation, my neighbors, or myself.
I am rarely able to receive your all-encompassing love.
Instead of fanning the flames of your love in my midst, too often I have quenched the divine sparks.
Instead of allowing your Holy Breath to swirl around me freely, sometimes
I have tried to trap the breeze in a box to be used for my own purposes.
I ask you to blow away the cobwebs of temptation and to blot out the stain of my offenses.
I pray that your light may shine through me, and I may become all you created me to be.
I hope that I may reflect your Glorious Harmony in the world.
I ask this in your Beautiful Names, O God of One Hundred Names,
but especially in the name of Jesus through the power of the Holy Spirit. Amen.

COLLECT FOR MORNING

Morning Star, as the sun moves through the heavens, night becomes day. As the Spirit moves through the world, the dusks and dawns of life become holy ground. May I feel the sparkle of your radiance so deeply within that I am able to live fully into this day. Let my spirit play in your presence, regardless of what transpires. For I pray in the name of the Sacred Three. Amen.

Prayers

Offer Personal Prayers and Thanksgiving.
Choose Collects from Parts Two, Three, or Four, as desired.

A Gift to the World

A chalice of milk was brought to me,
And I drank it in the sweetness of the kindness of the Lord.

The Son is the chalice,
And he who was milked is the Father,
And she who milked him is the Holy Spirit.

Because his breasts were full
And it was not beneficial to express his milk for no reason,

The Holy Spirit opened her bosom,
And mixed the milk of the Father's two breasts.

Then she gave the intimate mixture to the world without their knowing it.
And those who received it are in the fullness of the promise.

Hallelujah!

Odes of Solomon 19

IN PRAISE OF RELATIONSHIPS

For the singer whose voice sounds through the stillness, give thanks.
For the prayer partner whose hands tremble with the vitality of the Holy Spirit, give thanks.
For the soul-mate whose gentleness calms troubled souls, give thanks.
For the healer whose touch radiates heavenly heat, give thanks.
For the friend whose face reflects strength and determination, give thanks.
For all companions on the way, give thanks.
For angels among us, give thanks.

Todah Rabbah.
Shokran Katir.
Many Thanks.
For one and all to the All-in-All.

Three Things

I am the Lord your God.
To three things the Torah is compared:
To the wilderness,
To fire,
And to water.
This is to tell you that just as these are free to everyone coming into the world,
So the words of Torah are free to everyone coming into the world.

Mekhilta of Rabbi Ishmael's Bahodesh 5.IX

Closing

May the Light who lightens my life today illumine all of my tomorrows!

Midday Prayer

Greeting

Delight of my heart, rest in my peace; nestle into my presence.

JUSTICE

But let justice roll down like waters, and righteousness like an ever-flowing stream.

Amos 5:24

COLLECT FOR MIDDAY

Holy Mystery, you are the life force that courses through my soul. When my world is spinning like a top, cradle me in your arms like a newborn. When confusion abounds, be my compass. When I am caught up in a hurricane of activity, draw me into the eye, so I may find peace amidst the chaos. For I would so love to skip with you along life's byways. Amen.

Prayers

Offer Personal Prayers and Thanksgiving.
Choose Collects from Parts Two, Three, or Four, as desired.

WISDOM'S CALL

Does not wisdom call, and does not understanding raise her voice? On the heights, beside the way, at the crossroads she takes her stand; beside the gates in front of the town, at the entrance of the portals she cries out: "To you, O people, I call, and my cry is to all that live. O simple ones, learn prudence, acquire intelligence, you who lack it."

PROVERBS 8:1–5

SONG OF THE TREES

We are the Standing People.
We, trees with our leaves blowing in the breeze, are visible signs of that mighty wind, the Holy Breath, which hovered over the face of the earth
when it was void and without form.
We breathe in what you breathe out, and we give back fresh air, life.
Just as the Spirit can be a gentle breeze or a gale force wind,
we can give shade and life, or
we can conduct lightning to the ground, shocking whatever is beneath our branches.
We remember the souls that have flown to their creator during thunderstorms.
Wave with us to the Great Spirit of Life, the guide from this world to the next.
Ache with us over the destruction of so many of our family of trees.
Care for us as we care for you, in life and in death.
Wave with us in thanksgiving to the God of all of creation.

Glory to you who hovered,
Glory to you who blows,
Glory to you who guides.

SONG OF THE PHILLIPPIAN SLAVE GIRL, ACTS 16:16–19

I'm on my way in faith and hope.
No one can sway me or stand in my way.
I'm free, I'm free to do as I choose.
I'm off; I'm away to share the Good News!

I've been called a lot of things in my life.
To some people I'm a slave girl.
To others I'm a certain damsel.
To still others I'm a female slave.

One thing is certain:
Until that spirit was cast out of me, I had nothing.
  No freedom, no voice, no spiritual gifts, not even a name.
My owners owned my body,
  and that spirit controlled my mind, my will, even my voice.
No one even ever bothered to tell me my name!

But that's O.K.
I've named myself.
From here on out,
my name's Zoe
because by the time that I die
people are going to know that I lived!

Closing

All things are ripened by warmth just as all things are sanctified by the Spirit, O visible type.

St. Ephrem the Syrian's *Hymns of Faith 74.9*

Evening Prayer

Greeting

I was glad when they said to me, "Let's go Home to Mother's House."

WORDS OF COMFORT

For if John the Baptizer who was great called out, "I am not worthy to unfasten the straps of Your sandals, O Lord," then like the fearful woman, I must take refuge in the shadow of your garment, that I might be loosened from fear. And like that woman who was afraid and was comforted because she was healed, heal my awful trepidation, and I will be comforted by you. Let me pass from your garment to your body, so I may speak of your body according to my strength.

St. Ephrem the Syrian's *Hymns of Faith 10.5–6*

Collect for Evening

Divine Darkness, you separated the light from the darkness and pronounced both of them good. Our days and nights and twilight times are in your hands. Draw us close to you as evening approaches, so whether we wake or sleep or work or play, we rest wholly in you. For we pray in the name of the One who neither slumbers, nor sleeps, yet rested on the seventh day. Amen.

Prayers

Offer Personal Prayers and Thanksgiving.
Choose Collects from Parts Two, Three, or Four, as desired.

SONG OF SPIDER WOMAN

(Spider Woman is the Pan-Tribal Mother of domestic harmony and tranquility.)

I spin and I weave,
I spin and I weave
The center of my web;
I spin and I weave,
I spin and I weave
The center of my web,
Bearing my babies in my body as I weave,
Bearing my babies in my body as I weave.
I spin and I weave,
I spin and I weave
The center of my web.

I spin and I weave,
I spin and I weave
The middle of my web;
I spin and I weave,
I spin and I weave
The middle of my web,
Swaddling babies in gossamer silk as I go,
Swaddling babies in gossamer silk as I go.
I spin and I weave,
I spin and I weave
The middle of my web.

I spin and I weave,
I spin and I weave
The edges of my web;
I spin and I weave,
I spin and I weave
The edges of my web,
Waving as the weanlings in the wind fly away,
Waving as the weanlings in the wind fly away.
I spin and I weave,
I spin and I weave
The edges of my web.

I spin and I weave,
I spin and I weave
the center of my web.
I spin and I weave,
I spin and I weave
the middle of my web,
Preparing my web to start all over again,
Preparing my web to start all over again.
I spin and I weave,
I spin and I weave
the edges of my web.

MANY WOMBS

Creation conceived His symbols; Mary conceived His limbs.
Now many wombs have brought forth the Only-Begotten: Mary's womb brought him forth in pain, and also creation brought him forth in symbols.

ST. EPHREM THE SYRIAN'S *HYMN OF VIRGINITY 6.8.1–2*

AN AFFIRMATION OF FAITH

I believe that you, O God, created humanity, female and male, in your image.
I hear you, O Lord, and your call to love you with all my heart, with all my soul, with all my strength, and with all my mind, and your command to love my neighbors as myself.
I accept others, just as you have accepted me, in order to bring praise to you, O God.
I hope to shine like the stars in the universe as I hold out the word of life to my community.
I am committed to growing in your knowledge and love and to participating in the life of my faith community.
I praise you for removing my sackcloth and clothing me with yourself so that my heart may sing to you and not be silent.
I hope through Jesus the Risen One in the power of the Holy Spirit now and forever. Amen.

BASED ON GENESIS 1:26, MARK 12:29–31, ROMANS 15:7, PHILIPPIANS 2:15, ACTS 2:42, AND PSALMS 30:11–12.

Closing

May the Darkness that revitalizes my soul attune me to the Harmony of Creation.

PART TWO

Season Stories and Collects for Each Week of the Year

The China Cabinet: Display

As you move around the banquet table preparing your feast for the soul, feel free to select the plates and platters from the display part of the china cabinet that suit your needs. May these weekly Collects nourish your soul, while the Season Stories enhance your enjoyment of this spiritual banquet.

At the beginning of each season, there is a story of a woman—She Who Prays—who is the epitome of the qualities that are represented by the animals in the Collects. The story gives an overview of the progress of She Who Prays through her spiritual evolution. Following the story are the individual Collects for the season, one for each week, and following the Collects is a poem invoking the power of the qualities of the animals, plants, and minerals. Each quality is represented by the animal, the plant, and the mineral. For example, one quality is Transmutation, which can be represented by Aloe Vera and Moldavite as easily as by Snake. The combination of the animal, plant, and mineral is completed by the praying human to form a four-part microcosm of the Order of Creation, which appears in many expressions of Native American spirituality.

One note about communal use of the Collects: When the presider has said, "I have spoken," typical responses will be "Aho!" from men and "Eyah!" from women; if such native responses seem artificial, an appropriate response in English would be "It is good!" These Collects were prayerfully written at Patricia's altar on her front porch overlooking a pond visited by turtles, deer, bobcats, and coyotes, surrounded by trees visited by bluebirds, hawks, falcons, and eagles. May the reading of these Collects be a blessing to you.

SPRING: WISDOMSEEKER

The Wisdomseeker of the Spring, of the East, of new beginnings, of the maiden, is White Shell Woman. Among the tribes of the American Southwest, the young woman who is the bride wears the jewelry that shines iridescent in the sun. She welcomes what she is becoming, and she welcomes the changes in her life. For her people, she transforms the old energy and brings new energy into the community.

She is for them **Transmutation** (Snake), as she sloughs off the old skin.
She heals and balances and **Transforms** (Butterfly) the community's energy on her special day.
She is for them the **Rebirth** (Bat) of the goddess.
She is **Patient** (Ant) in her preparations as she experiences for the tribe again the old ceremonies of being prepared as a bride for her groom, and as she gathers the energy for the ultimate ceremony months, weeks, and days ahead.
She is a **Builder** (Beaver) of a new house and must prepare for her place in the community as the woman of the new home it will become.
She is a **Weaver** (Spider) of new garments and of new ceremonial cloth and of new life.
She is a **Messenger** (Hawk) from White Shell Woman, bringing the voice of the goddess again to life.

The young bride undergoes the positive changes in her life that are handed down through the ages from generation to generation, from mother to daughter to granddaughter to great-granddaughter, and as a result, she knows the goodness of **Migration** (Snow Goose), and she knows that changes bring **Integration** (Alligator) based on the **Integrity** (Jaguar), coming from the true center of her own **Wisdom** (Salmon), coming ultimately to her and through her to her community from the **Spirit** (Eagle).

May the aid, blessing, and company of all the wild Spring relatives be mine
and thine this season of renewal and new beginnings.

Week 1: Transmutation

Animal: Snake ***Plant: Aloe Vera*** ***Mineral: Moldavite***

Sacred Mystery, I stand before you this new day of a new year humbly asking your aid in shedding the skin of the old year, filled with the toxins of my weaknesses. Help me slip out of the old skin and glide into a new beginning, glistening and iridescent, powerful and capable of transmuting the poisons sent my way into not just benign substances, but into catalytic substances for changing my world. I am thankful to you for guidance this new day, this new year. I have spoken.

Week 2: Transformation

Animal: Butterfly ***Plant: Marigold*** ***Mineral: Fire Agate***

Grandfather Sun, I lift my arms to you this day, feeling your warmth like the butterfly emerging from the chrysalis, spreading her wings to dry in the light of your love. Thank you for this time of transformation in my life, of making changes in my life for my own good, knowing that those changes will change other lives and move through my world to make all our lives better. May my changes bring the gentle wind of new life to all whom I love and hold dear. I have spoken.

Week 3: Rebirth

Animal: Bat ***Plant: Lily of the Valley*** ***Mineral: Sodalite***

Grandmother Moon, you who shine your gentle light on all life below, thank you for shining your light on Bat's wings and granting us release from the old fruitless ways so that new life may come forth, growing from first emergence to maturity to completion and harvest. Thank you for rebirth in the quiet hours of the night. Thank you for nourishing our dreams, guiding us to their realization, and leading us to completing the cycle. I have spoken.

Week 4: Patience

Animal: Ant ***Plant: Daffodil*** ***Mineral: Herkimer Diamond***

I send a voice of thanksgiving to you, my little relative Ant, for teaching me the importance of patience, for teaching me to be methodical in cooperating with Life-Giving Spirit, for teaching me to have not only my needs but the needs of my family and my community in mind as I go about the day's work. Thank you for teaching me the true joy of generosity to others, for teaching me to trust that Sacred Mystery will provide for all our needs from the abundance of the Field of Plenty. I have spoken.

Week 5: Building

Animal: Beaver ***Plant: Red Clover*** ***Mineral: Abalone***

Thank you, my little relative Beaver, for teaching me the joys of industry, for showing me the delights of building a home sanctuary for my loved ones and for myself, for teaching me creative ways to escape the limitations that appear in the way. Thank you for showing me ingenious ways to escape setbacks and adversity, for protecting myself and those I love. Thank you for demonstrating the power of gnawing on one problem at a time and of balancing my priorities so that I am constantly aware of the dangers that exist, yet confident in my ability to meet those challenges successfully. I have spoken.

Week 6: Weaving

Animal: Spider ***Plant: Hollyhock*** ***Mineral: Garnet***

I send a voice of thanksgiving to you, Father Sun, for illuminating the dewy beads on Sister Spider's web this morning. I send a voice of thanksgiving to you, my little Sister Spider, for the iridescence of your beaded web that sparkles in the sunlight, reminding me that if I do my work, in due time, Spirit will decorate it with joy and cause that work to stand out in glory to the pleasure of my companions. Thank you, Great Spirit, for putting me in this place at this time to see the miraculous beauty of Great Mystery's creation. Thank you for the joy of work well done. I have spoken.

Week 7: Messenger

Animal: Hawk ***Plant: Iris*** ***Mineral: Lapis Lazuli***

Thank you, Brother Hawk, for drawing my attention to your beauty and power this day. Thank you for your message to be aware, to be observant, and to be watchful of all that surrounds me. Thank you for the lesson in seeing details, in looking at the big picture. Thank you for the encouragement to develop a keenness and boldness, to develop my own medicine, to accept my responsibilities, and to always seek the truth. Thank you for reminding me that I do have the abilities to overcome my difficulties, that I have my own power available to read the landscape of my life, and to prevail. I have spoken.

Week 8: Migration

Animal: Snow Goose ***Plant: Palm*** ***Mineral: Rhodochrosite***

I send a voice to you, Snow Goose, and to all our brothers and sisters flying with you to the snowfields of the North. May your trip home to the nesting areas be straight as the arrow of your flight this day. Thank you for bringing Father Sun back from the winter lands, helping the crops to grow abundantly for all the people. Thank you for your mysterious voice calling our hearts to acknowledge the turning of the Medicine Wheel of the Seasons, to encourage our own sisters and brothers as you do yours, and to send thanksgiving to Great Spirit with our own voices for the bountiful Field of Plenty that exists throughout this beautiful Turtle Island, our homeland. I have spoken.

Week 9: Integration

Animal: Alligator ***Plant: Angelica*** ***Mineral: Moonstone***

Thank you, my fearsome relative Alligator, whose reptile brain I share, for showing me how to bask in the sun and to glide into the water, integrating the pains and the pleasures of life, and teaching me to laugh at what angers me. Thank you for allowing me to see all the points of view I need to see so that I may make the best decisions possible. Thank you for reminding me to be flexible, to honor the progress I make, even though I may see the progress as slow-moving, even glacial. Thank you for inspiring me to seek the long view, to assess all my options, to acknowledge all my risks, to delight in the serendipitous unexpected, so that I may prevail not for myself alone, but also for my loved ones and for all the people. I have spoken.

Week 10: Integrity

Animal: Jaguar ***Plant: Pine*** ***Mineral: Amethyst***

Sister Jaguar, thank you for showing me how to purify myself of all uncleanliness and inappropriateness, so that I may honorably and lovingly use my influence and power for the right causes and in the right way. Thank you for counseling me to be kind, to serve compassionately, to open my heart and my soul to all those in need. Thank you for reminding me to act out of my deepest integrity, doing the best I can to maintain my own dignity and honesty and at the same time encouraging others to do so as well. Thank you for reminding me of the power of merciful forgiveness. Thank you for aiding me to walk gently and humbly on Mother Earth, doing what I have the power to do in correcting abuses of all kinds and striving for impeccable uprightness in all my relationships. I have spoken.

Week 11: Wisdom

Animal: Salmon ***Plant: Mulberry*** ***Mineral: Ruby***

I send a voice of grateful thanksgiving to you, my little relative Salmon, for reminding me to return to the Source of my creation. I thank you for calling me to remember my origins as one of Mother Earth's children, placed here on earth to seek wisdom, to view each event of my life as an assignment in wisdom, and to honor each relative I encounter as my teacher of wisdom. Thank you for reminding me of my ability to discern the flow of energies around me and to go against the flow that would take me away from the purpose of my life here on Mother Earth. Thank you for your assistance in maintaining a single-mindedness amid confusing distractions, helping me swim upstream following the quiet inner Voice of the purpose which Sacred Mystery has for me. I have spoken.

Week 12: Spirit

Animal: Eagle ***Plant: Sweetgrass*** ***Mineral: Sapphire***

I honor you, Brother Eagle, chief of the Winged Ones, gliding high among the Thunder Beings above me. I send a voice of humble respect to you, awed by your presence in my life this day, connecting me with Great Spirit and helping me see from your vast perspective. Little as I am, I honor your call to follow Great Spirit in my life, to soar above the mundane anxieties, burdens, confusions, and pains of my everyday life. Thank you for calling me to fly with you and with Great Spirit, as a co-creator of our adventure together circling around Mother Earth. Thank you for helping me, even with my broken wings, to fly in a straight path toward Great Spirit's healing medicine. I have spoken.

Invocation for Spring

By the transmutation of snake, aloe vera, and moldavite,
By the transformation of butterfly, marigold, and fire agate,
By the rebirth of bat, lily of the valley, and sodalite,
By the patience of ant, daffodil, and Herkimer diamond,
By the building of beaver, red clover, and abalone,
By the weaving of spider, hollyhock, and garnet,
By the message of hawk, iris, and lapis lazuli,
By the migrating of snow goose, palm, and rhodochrosite,
By the integration of alligator, angelica, and moonstone,
By the integrity of jaguar, pine, and amethyst,
By the wisdom of salmon, mulberry, and ruby,
By the spirit of eagle, sweetgrass, and sapphire,

May the aid, blessing, and company of all the wild Spring relatives be mine
and thine this season of renewal and new beginnings.

SUMMER: WISDOMBEARER

The Wisdombearer of the Summer, of the South, of growth and bearing fruit, of the young matron is the Corn Mother or the Maize Mother, who was known in many tribes as the embodiment of Mother Earth. It is said that so much sweet corn was cultivated by the tribes of America, just as contact was being made by the Europeans, that the sailors could smell the sweet corn on the wind for miles out into the Atlantic Ocean. The Maize Mother in her concerns for her children discerns and follows true dreams, not illusions or glamoring.

In her pregnancy, Maize Mother keeps her **Secrets** (Lynx), knowing of her coming labor of love.
She is wary of the humorous teachings of the **Trickster** (Coyote) who inquisitively sticks his nose in her business, and
She diligently **Scrutinizes** (Mouse) the wiles of the Trickster.
She is not afraid of **Confrontation** (Wild Boar) in protecting herself and her offspring.
She sees through **Illusion** (Dragonfly) which the Trickster conjures, and
she pays attention to the true **Dreaming** (Lizard) that Great Spirit instills in her, and follows the Dream's wisdom.
She acknowledges the true **Magic** (Raven) of wisdom and repudiates the false glamoring that the Trickster offers.
She knows deep within that wisdom comes from the sacred **Mystery** (Black Panther), and that the true place of discernment of answers and truth is within herself; her true teacher speaks with her own voice.
She prepares for the fruition of her labor by **Cleansing** (Frog) herself and her house.
She goes into a state of preoccupied **Introspection** (Bear) to find her way and the best for her children.
She knows that when **Boundaries** (Armadillo) have to be crossed, and when she experiences **Fear** (Rabbit), that she will have the **Protection** (Raccoon) that she needs and that she is completely capable of **Self-Protection** (Porcupine).
She awaits the Delivery and Birth of the product of her Labor, whether that product be baby or book or business. The Maize Mother is the fullness of summer.

May the aid, blessing, and company of all the wild Summer creatures be mine
and thine this season of growing.

Week 13: Secret-discerning

Animal: Lynx ***Plant: Red Rose*** ***Mineral: Clear Quartz***

Thank you, my little relative Lynx, for reminding me to keep the secrets that need to be kept until the proper time of sharing. Thank you for helping me to see and hear the secrets that Great Spirit sends me, secrets of anticipation, of joy, of waiting patiently until the right moment for disclosure or presentation or birth. Thank you for helping me not to let the cat out of the bag prematurely, spoiling the surprises Great Spirit has in store. Thank you, too, for helping me remember to keep safe all secrets revealed to me by my sisters and brothers so that trust and security are always a part of all my relationships. I have spoken.

Week 14: Trickster

Animal: Coyote ***Plant: Sycamore*** ***Mineral: Pyrite***

I send a voice of gratitude to you, my relative Coyote, for reminding me to laugh at myself! Thank you for your Trickster antics, for snooping around the boundaries of what I take too seriously. Thank you for revealing the healing medicine of comedy, not only in my own life, but in all my relationships with my loved ones, with my co-workers, with all my community. Thank you for the knots and snarls, the pranks, the trickery, and even the confusion that you bring, highlighting what is truly important and enduring in life. Thank you for cautioning me that what I send out into the world comes back to me multifold. Great Spirit, may all that I send out into the world be proper and acceptable to you. I have spoken.

Week 15: Scrutiny

Animal: Mouse ***Plant: Ivy*** ***Mineral: Copper***

Gratitude to you, my tiny relative Mouse, for encouraging me to look at life more closely and to scrutinize the details. Thank you for encouraging me to jump high in the attempt to see the Sacred Mountain that is difficult for the lowly and the humble to view easily. Thank you for advising me to take each adventure Spirit sends my way one step at a time until I arrive at a point where the mystery is made plain and the goal is within reach. Little as you are, you send wise counsel to those who would honorably walk the Good Red Road. I have spoken.

Week 16: Confrontational confidence

Animal: Wild Boar ***Plant: Fig*** ***Mineral: Obsidian***

Difficult as it is to thank you, Wild Boar, I do send a voice of thanksgiving for the way you assist me in the confrontations that I face. Thank you for calling me to stand up for myself, for my beliefs, for my loved ones, for all that I value and hold dear. Thank you for empowering me to be a warrior for just causes and for the downtrodden, and for showing me where I can correct the abuse and misuse of power and authority that I encounter. Thank you for reminding me that I do have the courage to face my weaknesses and helplessness and that I am put on Mother Earth for the purpose for which Great Spirit made me. I have spoken.

Week 17: Illusion-interpretation

Animal: Dragonfly ***Plant: Peach*** ***Mineral: Platinum***

Sister Dragonfly, I stand in awe of your beauty, shining iridescent in the light of Father Sun. Thank you, my little winged relative, for appearing in my life today, recalling to my mind that all may not be as it appears. Thank you for hovering over the places in my life that are not as they appear to be on the surface, so that I may rectify what needs perfecting. Thank you for sending news of renewing transformation, for reminding me of my own role in creating illusion, and for aiding me to co-create not more illusion but the true magical wonder of reality that Great Spirit constantly manifests. Thank you for your wise messages from the psychic realms this day. I have spoken.

Week 18: Dreaming

Animal: Lizard ***Plant: Lupine*** ***Mineral: Jasper***

Greetings to you, Brother Lizard, for moving from the Dreamtime into my reality this day. Thank you for your messages from the Dreamland and for your revelation of the Shadow areas of my life. Thank you for going with me into the nightmare as well as into the joyous dream, and thank you for counseling me to create the joy and not the fear. I send a voice of deep gratitude to you for the marvelous tool of the dream in realizing the joy I would create not only for myself and my loved ones, but also for my community and for all people everywhere. I have spoken.

Week 19: Magic-making

Animal: Raven ***Plant: Holly*** ***Mineral: Opal***

My relative Raven, I stand in wonder at your magical powers to move from Sacred Mystery through all generations and all time to the present, calling me to ceremony, to the ritual of healing my fears and exorcizing my demons. I send a voice of gratitude to you for accompanying me into this place of healing as I learn to walk more righteously the Good Red Road before me. I am grateful for the creative gifts you provide—the gifts of insight, of courage, of willingness to be healed and to heal. I am humbly thankful for your conveying the healing creative energy Flow from the Sacred Mystery into my life this day. I have spoken.

Week 20: Mystery

Animal: Black Panther ***Plant: Walnut*** ***Mineral: Fluorite***

Magnificent Black Panther, I, humble as I am, truly thank you for manifesting yourself in my life this day. I am grateful for your company as I face the fears and darkness of my Shadow. I am thankful for your aid in bringing to Light all the interior places in my life that need to be healed. I am grateful for your counsel to face my darkness with courage, knowing that I can trust Great Spirit in this journey toward Wholeness and Holiness. I send a voice of gratitude to you for helping me clean out the trash in my soul and spirit so that I may more honorably walk the Good Red Road that Great Spirit calls me to travel. I have spoken.

Week 21: Cleansing

Animal: Frog ***Plant: Sage*** ***Mineral: Rutilated Quartz***

Thank you, my little relative Frog for calling to the Thunder Beings to come cleanse Mother Earth. I, too, need cleansing. Thank you for inspiring those ceremonies that purify guilt, fatigue, weakness, and emptiness. Thank you for your assistance in getting rid of the negative distractions of my life, in sealing off the energy drains that would enervate me, in removing obstacles that prevent me from walking the Good Red Road. I send a voice of thanksgiving to you for reminding me that renewal and refreshment are at hand and readily available, that all I need do is send a voice of request for aid. Thank you, also, for company as I move into a time and a place of greater energy and brighter light. I have spoken.

Week 22: Introspection

Animal: Bear ***Plant: Flowering Fern*** ***Mineral: Labradorite***

Thanksgiving to you, Sister Bear, for calling me to introspective hibernation. I am grateful for a time of rest, a time of rejuvenation, a time of return to Mother Earth for replenishing and recharging. Thank you for the fallow times that precede creativity and growth, for the generative quiet and gentle darkness that precede the bursting forth of new life. Thank you for tranquil places where nurture provides new direction and new inspiration. Thank you for plentiful times of relaxation and recreation so that I might have the insight and the stamina to realize the dreams that call to me in the night. Thank you, my relative, for taking my message of gratitude to Great Spirit this day for all the blessings of this life. I have spoken.

Week 23: Boundary-making

Animal: Armadillo ***Plant: Morning Glory*** ***Mineral: Hematite***

I send a voice of thanksgiving to you, my little relative Armadillo, for crawling into my life, reminding me to set boundaries that cannot be trespassed. I am grateful for your counsel to call on my medicine power to protect and shield myself and my loved ones. Thank you for reminding me of my vulnerabilities, and for helping me to use those vulnerabilities for good and not for wrong. Thank you for helping me discern where others would abuse their power and authority for selfish ends, and for aiding me in avoiding the absorption of the negativity engendered by such abuse. May I, like you, be a companion in need to those who fall victim to such abuse. I have spoken.

Week 24: Fear-defeating

Animal: Rabbit ***Plant: Amaryllis*** ***Mineral: Aquamarine***

Little relative Rabbit, I appreciate this day the fear that freezes you in midstep. I, too, have felt such paralyzing fear, stopped dead in my tracks at the enormity of the threat. I send a voice of thanksgiving to you, for recalling to me that fear and that paralysis. May we both learn to breathe into the fear and to find within ourselves the capability of moving in a direction of true sanctuary and defense. May we both learn to release our handicapping fears into Mother Earth who is capable of transforming the toxicities of our timidity into courage to face our enemies and to prevail over them. I have spoken.

Week 25: Protection

Animal: Raccoon ***Plant: Juniper*** ***Mineral: Turquoise***

Gratitude to you, my relative Raccoon, for aid in providing those I love with a place of protection. I am thankful to you for calling up from me the warrior who protects not only her own loved ones, but all the young, all the elderly, all the infirm who are incapable of protecting themselves. I am grateful to you for reminding me to give back to Sacred Mystery the gifts of strength, of guidance, and of sanctuary that I have received in my past. Thank you for reminding me that in the days of our ancestors only the truly valorous warriors were chosen to protect the babies, the mothers, the grandmothers, and the grandfathers in time of enemy attack. May I prove to be strong and successful in my defense of those who need defending. I have spoken.

Week 26: Self-protection

Animal: Porcupine ***Plant: Mountain Ash*** ***Mineral: Carnelian***

Thank you, my wonderfully made little Sister Porcupine, for reminding me this day that the protector also needs to protect herself. I am thankful to you for revealing to me the need to hold defense in reserve even while being open, honest, and sharing with others. I am grateful to you for giving me permission to use that defense in time of need when negotiation fails, for giving good counsel that martyrdom may not be necessary. I send a voice of thanksgiving, especially, for showing me that I may reveal my vulnerabilities when appropriate because I do have the capacity to protect myself from those who would take advantage of what they perceive as weakness in me. I have spoken.

Invocation for Summer

By the secret-discerning of lynx, red rose, and clear quartz,
By the humorous trickster teachings of coyote, sycamore, and pyrite,
By the scrutinizing of mouse, ivy, and copper,
By the confrontational confidence of wild boar, fig, and obsidian,
By the illusion-interpretation of dragonfly, peach, and platinum,
By the dreaming of lizard, lupine, and jasper,
By the magic-making of raven, holly, and opal,
By the mysteriousness of black panther, walnut, and fluorite,
By the cleansing of frog, sage, and rutilated quartz,
By the introspection of bear, flowering fern, and labradorite,
By the boundary-making of armadillo, morning glory, and hematite,
By the fear-defeating of rabbit, amaryllis, and aquamarine,
By the protection of raccoon, juniper, and turquoise,
By the self-protection of porcupine, mountain ash, and carnelian,

May the aid, blessing, and company of all the wild Summer creatures
be mine and thine this growing season.

AUTUMN: WISDOMGIVER

The Wisdomgiver of the Fall, of the West, of harvesting, of the experienced matron is Spider Woman, yet another embodiment of the goddess who is profligate in providing for those who come to her in need, constantly giving and nurturing and comforting her children, bountifully expending her creative energy for the benefit of the whole community. She knows that harvesting is very hard work.

But, she knows that she has the **Stamina** (Elk) and strength to gather the harvest in.

She is constantly in **Action** (Antelope), and the action that she takes in **Hunting** (Weasel) is not an action of cruelty but one of necessity; she takes only what is needed for the continuation of her family and community.

She is careful to **Camouflage** (Fox) herself in hunting, and she is cautious concerning the camouflage of the hunted.

She is grateful for the **Sharing** of Owl who helps her see those who would mislead her.

She takes only what she needs from the **Abundance** (Buffalo) of the Field of Plenty and is not greedy; she leaves resources for others who need them. She is gentle with Mother Earth, who must provide not only for her, but for the next seven generations.

In her hunting and **Gathering** (Squirrel), she takes enough to provide for the needy who cannot hunt or gather for themselves, in order to honor the **Give-Away** (Turkey).

In her **Nurturance** (Turtle), she provides for those who depend on her and generously gives to those who need charity.

She is the spirit of **Gentleness** (Deer) and humility in providing for those who are her responsibility, remembering the times when she was needy and someone else provided for her.

She is the spirit of **Grace** (Swan) in giving away to the needy, allowing them dignity in their need.

She knows that the best **Teacher** (Wolf) is gentle with her students, and the best exercise of **Power** (Horse) is one that remembers to allow each child his or her own dignity.

May the aid, blessing, and company of all the wild Autumn creatures be mine and thine this harvest season.

Week 27: Stamina

Animal: Elk ***Plant: Cedar*** ***Mineral: Selenite/Gypsum***

Sister Elk, I send a voice of thanksgiving to you for reminding me to pace myself and not to outrun my strength, allowing me to expend the available energy I have to the maximum extent without burning out. I am grateful to you for these lessons in stamina. I am thankful, too, for the model you provide in finding strength and renewal among friends of my own gender; thank you for my companions who, following your Tribe's example, lift me up and support me. I am grateful to you, also, for the reminder to find joy and completion in mating with my partner, allowing us both release and renewal. For all these blessings in relationship—with myself, with my sisters, and with my brothers—I send a voice of deep gratitude. I have spoken.

Week 28: Action-taking

Animal: Antelope ***Plant: Thyme*** ***Mineral: Onyx***

Thank you, my fast-moving relative Antelope, for your counsel to act and to do. I am thankful for your aid in making those actions that I perform mindful, conscious, and knowledgeable, finding favor with Great Spirit and the ultimate plan Sacred Mystery has for all Creation. I appreciate your good example of acting quickly, decisively, and properly, in order to accomplish efficiently and effectively the purpose Great Spirit has for me as I travel the Good Red Road. I am grateful for your aid in solving knotty problems and circumventing obstructive impediments that I encounter on my path. I am especially thankful for your assistance as I act on behalf of my loved ones, my two-legged community, and all my relatives. I have spoken.

Week 29: Hunting

Animal: Weasel ***Plant: Forsythia*** ***Mineral: Rhodonite***

I am grateful to you, Weasel, for your lessons in hunting: to be watchful, to be persistent, to chase my prey, whatever it is, to the capture. Thank you for the encouragement to go into the tight places, to walk where no one else would dare go, in pursuit of what I seek. Thank you, too, for reminding me to move with silent stealth until the right moment. I am grateful for your help in searching out the secrets of my own power and in keeping those secrets to myself until the proper occasion for revelation. I appreciate your wise counsel to be vigilant, teaching me how to sidestep what would hinder my achieving the goals Great Spirit has for me, my loved ones, and my community. I send a voice of joyful gratitude for the reminder that, like your robe, my robe changes with the seasons to protect me as I hunt for Great Spirit's purpose in my life. I have spoken.

Week 30: Camouflage

Animal: Fox ***Plant: Coriander*** ***Mineral: Alexandrite***

Gratitude to you, my relative Fox, for reminding me to disguise myself, to change my robe in order to disappear into my environment so that I may observe the lay of the land before I act. Thank you for modeling the adaptability that I need to be successful in providing for myself, for my loved ones, and for those in my community who are needy. Thank you for helping me move silently and invisibly like the wind through situations that demand acute discernment. I am grateful for your lessons in becoming one with my world so that I can predict where the Flow of Great Spirit leads. Thank you for pointing out to me the places of hidden worth within myself and for encouraging me to observe with open eyes the hidden worth in those around me. May I always be helpful and supportive of those who need my counsel. I have spoken.

Week 31: Sharing

Animal: Owl ***Plant: White Cherry*** ***Mineral: Emerald***

I honor you, my relative Owl, for your ability to pierce the darkness with your sharp eyesight and hearing. I am thankful to you for your help in seeing behind the disguises to the truth that Great Spirit would have me see. I appreciate the wise messages of regeneration and enlightenment that you bring to me in dreams and visions. Thank you for your company in the dark that would terrify and overwhelm me, and thank you for asking who I am at regular intervals—I would be a courageous walker of the Good Red Road. I am grateful for your lessons in following my purpose silently and steadfastly, even when the pathway is difficult to discern. I honor your ability to share your territory with our diurnal relatives the hawks, demonstrating the importance of cooperation as we all cycle through the Medicine Wheel of the Seasons. I have spoken.

Week 32: Abundance

Animal: Buffalo ***Plant: Potato*** ***Mineral: Green Tourmaline***

Great relative Buffalo, I send a voice of respectful gratitude to you for your lessons in providing abundantly. I am grateful for the stories of your humble give-away in which all parts of your body were used by our ancestors for food, for clothing, and for shelter, not one part of your body wasted, all used to provide abundantly and generously for those who were in need. Such benevolence is unsurpassed on Mother Earth. I am thankful to you for your role in teaching us to pray and in creating community for us in time of needy exile. May I always remember your magnanimous sacrifice and, humble as I am, waste nothing of my physical energy, mental acuity, psychological adeptness, or spiritual holiness, using all for the benefit of my loved ones and of those in need. I have spoken.

Week 33: Gathering

Animal: Squirrel ***Plant: Corn*** ***Mineral: Gold***

Busy relative Squirrel, I honor your energy and diligence in gathering your provender for the approaching fallow time. I honor your wisdom in planning ahead and preparing for change. I thank you for the wise lessons in storing riches in many safe places, not just in one, so that provision is always close at hand. I send a voice of gratitude to Mother Earth for providing generously for both of us in this harvest-time from the abundant Field of Plenty. I honor you, Sacred Mystery, for the efficiency of inspiring my relative Squirrel to store acorns in Mother Earth so that some of the profligate bounty of seeds may grow new oak trees to feed and shelter our descendants down to the Seventh Generation. I have spoken.

Week 34: Give-away

Animal: Turkey ***Plant: Orange Tree*** ***Mineral: Bloodstone***

I honor you, my self-sacrificing relative Turkey, for your ultimate give-away this season of harvest and of thanksgiving. Your generosity models for us all the ability to martyr ourselves for the benefit of others so that the people might live. I send a voice of gratitude to all my relatives—military personnel, law enforcement agents, emergency rescue and medical workers—standing ready to sacrifice themselves in the service of others, keeping us safe while putting themselves in danger. Great Spirit, may such willingness to sacrifice self not be in vain, but for the ultimate benefit of all people who would walk humbly and righteously the path of good will, shared communion, and charitable community. I have spoken.

Week 35: Nurturance

Animal: Turtle ***Plant: Pineapple*** ***Mineral: Smoky Quartz***

Honor to you, Turtle, as the symbol for our portion of Mother Earth, Turtle Island, our homeland. I thank you for your lesson in protection, of going within ourselves when threatened with attack in order to discover the source of our defense. I honor you for your ability to live both in the Water World and on the earth. I am grateful to you for your example of carrying your home with you, so that wherever I go on this Mother Earth, I may lodge not with strangers but with brothers and sisters. May I, like you, come to be at home wherever my path leads. I have spoken.

Week 36: Gentleness

Animal: Deer ***Plant: Baby's Breath*** ***Mineral: Blue Quartz***

Thank you, Deer, for the reminder to walk in faith with gentleness wherever and with whomever my path leads. I honor your ability to trust in the good will of all companions, to love all people just as they are at the moment and, thereby calling from them the cooperation and nurturance that gentleness inspires. I am grateful for your joyful, fearless presence, inspiring that love and compassion that is always the proper answer to threats and attacks. May I learn to trust and to love unconditionally all my sisters and brothers walking with me, whether short distance or long, on the Good Red Road. May we all move toward a time of peace, beauty, and harmony where gentleness is the common way of behaving toward all our relatives. I have spoken.

Week 37: Grace

Animal: Swan ***Plant: Yellow Jasmine*** ***Mineral: Jade***

Graceful Swan, I enjoy your company this day, modeling for me the lesson to surrender to the transformation that Great Spirit makes a part of my very being. Thank you for the example demonstrating that perceived ugliness is transitory, that graceful beauty is an integral part of my natural makeup. I am grateful to you for calling me to accept the healing transformation with grace, to be fearless in the face of radical change that will only make my spirit more beautiful. Thank you, Great Spirit, for Swan's guidance as I learn to feel the eternal rhythms of Mother Earth, and to trust in the intuitive compulsions that lead me to follow the spirit Flow toward Sacred Mystery's ultimate purpose for my life. I have spoken.

Week 38: Teacher

Animal: Wolf ***Plant: Olive Tree*** ***Mineral: Coral***

I send a voice of gratitude to you, Wolf, for being a pathfinder on my journey. I honor you as my teacher in proper relationships within my community, urging me to take up my unique role in the human pack with whom I run. Thank you for encouraging me to share my strengths and my viewpoints cooperatively for the well-being of all our relatives. I am grateful for your example of following the Path to Great Spirit, of aiding me and accompanying me in my

Vision Quests. May I always humbly and honestly follow your example to do my very best for my companions while fostering my own integrity, so that our celebratory chorus may always be joyful. I have spoken.

Week 39: Power

Animal: Horse ***Plant: Mistletoe*** ***Mineral: Pearl***

Thanksgiving to you, Horse, for your powerful beauty trotting alongside me this day. I am grateful for your lessons in the use of power. Thank you for reminding me that those whose authority is most powerful are those leaders who truly care, who wear loving compassion as a robe in every event of life. I thank you for encouraging me to share the wisdom I have learned in my life's journey, to teach the lessons I have successfully fulfilled in walking the Good Red Road. I also honor you, Horse, for your role in carrying ceremonial leaders to Great Spirit's healing place in order to bring back powerful medicine, helping the wounded walk whole and holy once more. I have spoken.

Invocation for Autumn

By the stamina of elk, cedar, and selenite,
By the action-taking of antelope, thyme, and onyx,
By the hunting of weasel, forsythia, and rhodonite,
By the camouflage of fox, coriander, and alexandrite,
By the sharing of owl, white cherry, and emerald,
By the abundance of buffalo, potato, and green tourmaline,
By the gathering of squirrel, corn, and gold,
By the give-away of turkey, orange tree, and bloodstone,
By the nurturance of turtle, pineapple, and smoky quartz,
By the gentleness of deer, baby's breath, and blue quartz,
By the grace of swan, yellow jasmine, and jade,
By the teaching of wolf, olive tree, and coral,
By the power of horse, mistletoe, and pearl,

May the aid, blessing, and company of all the wild Autumn
creatures be mine and thine this harvest season.

WINTER: WISDOMKEEPER

The Wisdomkeeper of the Winter, of the North, of the fallow time, of the crone is White Buffalo Calf Woman, who brought the Seven Ceremonies to the Lakota. She is wise and venerable, bringing with her the traditions that must be kept, even in changed and changing circumstances. The bundle she carries has the Agent by which in our humility we may approach even the Great Mystery in dignity and need, humbly requesting benevolence, receiving that benevolence of grace, and praising the Source of all Creation. She knows that if we follow our "Teacher"—that innate Teacher of Wisdom within each of us—and develop ourselves, we will reach a place where true choice can be made.

She has the **Self-Esteem** (Moose) to be humble, and she is courageous enough to defend her position and to defend those who rely on her.
She has the **Persistence** (Blue Jay) and the **Assertiveness** (Badger) to follow her goals to their successful ends.
She has the **Respect** (Skunk) of being a wise counselor and of making just decisions.
She operates from a position of **Independence** (Cat), uncowed by special interests that are unworthy.
She embodies wise **Leadership** (Mountain Lion) and her sense of **Loyalty** (Dog) is to her own integrity and the counsel of wisdom within. She is concerned not only for herself and her children, but also for her children's children, down to the Seventh Generation.
She espouses **Lawfulness** (Crow) that is livable and just and fair, and not oppressive and separatist and discriminatory.
She knows that **Tradition** (Whale) is the way by which we have operated in the past but more than that, it is the way we learn to operate in the present and the way that our children and our children's children will operate down to the Seventh Generation.
She knows that anything is possible and acceptable as long as it hurts no one.
She is ready for the **Recreation** (Opossum) and celebration of her life, of life in general, and, like a grandmother with her babies, is full of **Playfulness** (Otter); she understands the importance of humor even in the most serious of circumstances.
She is full of **Joy** (Hummingbird) as she dances the **Sacred Dance** (Grouse) of a life rightly lived.

May the aid, blessing, and company of all the wild Winter creatures be mine and thine this fallow season of the year.

Week 40: Self-esteem

Animal: Moose ***Plant: Strawberry*** ***Mineral: Moss Agate***

Thank you, my relative Moose, for your joyful encouragement. I honor your delight in accomplishment, and I am grateful for your urging me to find delight in my own accomplishments. I send a voice of thanksgiving to Great Spirit for your wise counsel to rejoice, without feelings of self-negation, not only in my own victories, but also in the victories of my loved ones and my co-workers. May we always remember that joyfully spontaneous appreciation in doing our work well is more befitting those who walk the Good Red Road than grudging, selfish envy. May our joy, like yours, be an example to all who watch us succeed. I have spoken.

Week 41: Persistence

Animal: Blue Jay ***Plant: Water Willow*** ***Mineral: Aventurine***

I honor you, my noisy little relative Blue Jay, for combining the colors of Father Sky and Mother Earth in your robe. Thank you for your masterful combination of the energies sent by both our Father and our Mother. I send a voice of thanksgiving to you for your gift of persistence in the proper use of power and in your example of refusing to be victimized by the misuse of authority. I honor you for your resourcefulness and adaptability and for your tendency to solve the problems you face creatively, balancing the practical and the mysterious at the same time. Thank you for your teasing humor and self-confidence. May I follow your lead and find such easy delight in the use of my own talents. I have spoken.

Week 42: Assertiveness

Animal: Badger ***Plant: St. John's Wort*** ***Mineral: Black Tourmaline***

Gratitude to you, my relative Badger, for showing me that assertiveness is sometimes required to get my purpose accomplished. Thank you for your intrepid courage in setting your goals and reaching them, overcoming all who would stand in your way. I am grateful even for your grumpiness in attaining your objectives, for that grumpiness merely demonstrates the assured conviction of the rightness of your path. I honor you for your stubborn ambition in getting your job done and for your ability to creatively outsmart your enemies. May I, following your example, learn to ground myself in Mother Earth so that I have the endurance to attain my goals in life. I have spoken.

Week 43: Respect

Animal: Skunk ***Plant: Date*** ***Mineral: Tiger Eye***

Honor to you, my little relative Skunk, for your insistence on being respected. I am grateful to you for your lessons in knowing when others have transgressed personal boundaries and your ability to warn intruders without seriously harming them. Thank you for your demonstrations of self-knowledge and self-respect, of setting limits, and of communicating those limits by means of natural consequence. I am thankful for your demonstrating belief in self and pride in accomplishment, modeling for me that ultimate self-defense need not be irreparably damaging. May I learn to warn those who would drain my energy as forcibly, yet as harmlessly, as you. I have spoken.

Week 44: Independence

Animal: Cat ***Plant: Live Oak*** ***Mineral: Chrysoprase***

I am grateful to you, my independent relative Cat, for your lessons in living, for your mysteriousness, for your curiosity, for your cleverness, and for your delightful unpredictability. I honor you for the esteem you have commanded throughout the ages that you have associated with us two-leggeds, for your dignity that raised you to deity in the past as goddess of healing, of fertility, and of childbirth. I honor you, also, for your inquisitiveness in ceremony, for your fascination with the drum and the rattle. I am grateful for your company in ritual and your playful participation in maintaining the altars, even becoming part of the altar yourself! May I, like you, be a welcomed guest on the altar of Mother Earth. I have spoken.

Week 45: Leadership

Animal: Mountain Lion ***Plant: Scotch Fir*** ***Mineral: Topaz***

Thanksgiving to you, my relative Mountain Lion, for your leadership counsel. I honor you for going where your path leads without requiring followers to travel the same path. I honor you for showing me how to be an effective leader without depleting my energy. I honor you for following your heart's desires without imposing those desires on others. I honor you for guiding without encouraging dependency. Like you, I desire to accept my own responsibilities, communicate my own truth, and live in balance with all my brothers and sisters. May I, too, know instinctively those times when I need fellowship with my own kind and those times best spent in solitude. May I intuitively know those times that demand swift-moving authority and those periods of obligatory rest, so that my energy is spent wisely and never totally consumed. I have spoken.

Week 46: Loyalty

Animal: Dog *Plant: Bluebell* *Mineral: Malachite*

I am thankful to you, my constant relative and best friend, Dog, for your watching over me and guarding me, especially in the dark hours of the night. I send a voice of special thanksgiving to Great Spirit for your loyal faithfulness as I walk the Good Red Road. Thank you for your cheerful service, fierce protection, and loving companionship; your presence allows me a confidence that I might not have without you. May I always be to my friends as devoted and loyal as you are to me. Would that all two-leggeds were capable of such devotion and fidelity to each other in our walk on Mother Earth. I have spoken.

Week 47: Lawfulness

Animal: Crow *Plant: Dandelion* *Mineral: Silver*

Thank you, Crow, for your message today to always follow the law in all my activities. Thank you for reminding me not only of human political laws and loving relationship laws, but also of sacred laws. May I follow all of these laws, not only for my own sake, but also for the sake of my loved ones and for all the people I encounter on my path. May I always see each person as my brother or sister, my mother or father, my son or daughter. May I always wish only the best for each person I meet. May I always be willing to help and protect where help and protection are needed and to encourage where courage is faint. May I always walk the Good Red Road in charity, seeing each of my relatives as an honored teacher sent from Great Spirit. I have spoken.

Week 48: Tradition

Animal: Whale *Plant: Magnolia* *Mineral: Diamond*

Gratitude to you, my giant relative Whale, for keeping the records of tradition, for demonstrating with your own body that it is possible for air-breathing creatures to live in other environments. May I be able to live in Spirit as easily as you, originally a landwalker, live in water. Thank you for your powerful ability to broadcast your song over vast distances. I would, like you, sing my Spirit song so that all my relatives may hear the message of love and harmony that exists in the Spirit life. I send a voice of thanksgiving to Great Spirit for your realizing the importance of sound in offering gratitude for all the blessings that come to us from the Field of Plenty. May I always be as willing as you to sing my part in the Great Chorus. I have spoken.

Week 49: Recreation

Animal: Opossum ***Plant: Hyacinth*** ***Mineral: Sugalite***

I am grateful to you, my little relative Opossum, for your reminder to "play possum" when enemies would overcome me, allowing me to live to play again. Thank you, too, for your wise counsel to play out my plans before executing them so that I may perfect them before they come to exist in my world. I am thankful to you for your example of good strategy, of lying low when the odds are unfavorable, of waiting until advantage appears and victory is possible. I send a voice of thanksgiving for your advice, when I am in danger of burning out, to retreat into rest and recreation so that I may return to my struggles with renewed strength and energy, insuring my own victory and that of those for whom I am an advocate. I have spoken.

Week 50: Playfulness

Animal: Otter ***Plant: Parsley*** ***Mineral: Peridot***

Joyful thanksgiving to you, my playful little relative Otter, for enticing me to play. Thank you for reminding me that the play of a child is concentrated and serious and necessary for harmonious living. May I, when I have the opportunity to play with a child, join in that imaginative concentration and recover the wonder of childhood. Thank you for permission to play when others in my world demand work. I am grateful for those on my path who also see the necessity of playing, knowing that the most creative solutions to the problems we face are frequently given in a burst of inspiration during play, not in strenuous duties. I send a voice of gratitude to Great Spirit for the part Holy Play has in the Flow of Sacred Mystery. I have spoken.

Week 51: Joy

Animal: Hummingbird ***Plant: Wood Sorrel*** ***Mineral: Citrine***

Beautiful Hummingbird, I send a voice of wondering gratitude to you for your encouragement to seek joy and beauty as I walk the Good Red Road. I am thankful to you for your role in causing flowers to propagate, beautifying the world for all your relatives. Thank you for opening our hearts to this good day full of vibrant color and soothing music, bringing delight and refreshment to all your companions. Great Spirit, I thank you for the gift of this tiny relative who sends such a powerful message of hope and harmony. May I always, like this tiny creature, remember that no matter how humble, how little I am, my part is just as necessary in fulfilling the purposes of the Great Sacred Mystery. I have spoken.

Week 52: Sacred Dance

Animal: Grouse ***Plant: Yellow Lily*** ***Mineral: Amazonite***

I send a voice of thanksgiving to you, Grouse, for your lessons in dancing the Spiral Dance, spiraling in to the center and back out again, the dance of beginning and ending, of withdrawal and return, of birth and rebirth, reflecting the marvelous structure of the DNA in the tiniest cells and of the immense galaxies in the far-reaching universe. I am grateful for the hands of my partners as we step in rhythm to Mother Earth's heartbeat, performing our part of the Sacred Dance on the Medicine Wheel of Life. I am grateful for the celebrations of joy, of light, of love, of laughter as we circle in to our Source and back out to carry the message of peace, of justice, of equality, and of harmony to all our relatives. May we always, eternally, step in rhythm to Sacred Mystery's drumbeat. I have spoken.

Invocation for Winter

By the self-esteem of moose, strawberry, and moss agate,
By the persistence of blue jay, water willow, and aventurine,
By the assertiveness of badger, St. John's wort, and black tourmaline,
By the respect of skunk, date, and tiger's eye,
By the independence of cat, live oak, and chrysoprase,
By the leadership of mountain lion, scotch fir, and topaz,
By the loyalty of dog, bluebell, and malachite,
By the lawfulness of crow, dandelion, and silver,
By the tradition of whale, magnolia, and diamond,
By the recreation of opossum, hyacinth, and sugalite,
By the playfulness of otter, parsley, and peridot,
By the joy of hummingbird, wood sorrel, and citrine,
By the sacred dance of grouse, yellow lily, and amazonite,

May the aid, blessing, and company of all the wild Winter creatures
be mine and thine this fallow season of the year.

PART THREE

Prayers for Hearth and Home and Beyond

The China Cabinet: Drawers and Cupboards

Beneath the display in the china cabinet are the drawers and cupboards. These are the special nutrients that may be added to your feast whenever they are needed. The drawers and cupboards contain prayers that touch on some of the aspects of a woman's life, both ordinary and momentous. May they strengthen and encourage you to see the Open-handed One in every part your life.

ON GIVING

FOR COOKING

Great Spirit, I send a voice of deep gratitude to you for providing so abundantly and generously from the Field of Plenty for my guests, for all of my loved ones, and for me. I honor you, my relative (name the animal providing the meat for the meal), for your ultimate give-away so that we may live. I also thank you my plant relatives (name the vegetables, fruits, and grains) for adding to the nourishment of our lives. Thank you plants that provide drinks and dairy animals that provide products so that we are well-fed and healthy. I am grateful to you all this day.

FOR GIVING GOODS TO CHARITY

Great Spirit, I send a voice of thanksgiving to you for blessing me with an abundance of clothing, shoes, books, household goods, and decorative items. As I pack each item into boxes I recall the good service each performed for me and I remember the joy it has brought to my life. But these goods, once important, no longer grow corn in my life, so I send them forth into the world to benefit others who will find good use for them. May they enjoy these objects as much as I have. Thank you for providing so generously from the vast Field of Plenty.

FOR HOPE FOR A PARENT OF TEENAGERS

When you were wee and so full of glee,
  I wished for so much:
For time to love, time to see
  Just how much you mean to me.

Now you're old, O so old,
  Soon to be ump-teen,
  And life can seem so mean.

I wish for so much:
For a salve to heal our souls
  of the cuts and bruises we've sustained
    in our journey from your birth to here-and-now.

With the love in my heart,
And the Spirit in my soul,
I say: "Let's wipe away the tears together,"
And some fine day we'll remember all this and say:
"We made it! C'est la vie!"

FOR A MOTHER IN DISTRESS: PART I

Motherly Father, "into your hands I commend my daughter."
She's so beautiful, so giving, so naïve.
As one mother to another, I need to say,
"I'm so afraid for her."
Not for her physical health, as much as for her emotional, spiritual
  well-being.
She is being torn to shreds,
Head going one way, heart holding on for dear life to her prize,
  a boyfriend.
Soul being swamped by raging hormones.
Lord, have mercy on her soul, bone of my bone, flesh of my flesh.

Christ, have mercy on his soul, a young man not so different from
  you once.
Lord, have mercy on me, a fear-filled Mom,
  With a hope-filled girl within, and
  A love-filled woman.
Into your hands, Mother, I commend myself,
Into your hands, Father, I commend my daughter and her beau.

FOR A MOTHER IN DISTRESS: PART II

Father, "into your hands I commend my spirit,"
So you said from the cross, Dear Jesus.
Father-Mother, into your hands I commend my daughter,
As she goes off to college,
As our family changes beyond recognition.
This mothering thing is hard work,
And I'm just now beginning to get it right,
  Some of the time.
But you, Great God, created her well, and
  You got it right.
Yes, into your hands I commend my daughter,
My hopes, my fears, my smiles, my tears.
Keep loving her, Loving God, even more than I do.

FOR MOVING (NEW JOB/MILITARY/UNIVERSITY/MINISTRY)

As our daughter (son) leaps out of the nest, watch over her (him) in her new life (job, military, university, etc.). Soothe the aches and pains of our family life with the aloe vera of your Holy Spirit. Through the rough waters generated by the generation gap remind us of the good times as you guide us through the peaks and troughs of everyday life. Shower your healing presence on us so abundantly that by the time she/he moves, we've re-connected enough to act, not only as a safety net for her (him) to fall back on, but also as a trampoline from which she can spring forward. Amen.

FOR CONTINUITY AND CONNECTION

God our Mother and Father,
When people I love and total strangers utter words of brokenness,
  strengthen your hold on me.
"The family line won't continue
    if you don't get married,
    if you don't marry the 'right' kind of person,

if the two of you can't make a baby,
if you don't have a son . . ."
Enough!

Good God of Love,
Ease the fear I have of letting people down.
There was a time when people believed that life was in the blood,
and it meant the right to a man's name, an identity.
Well, life is still in the blood, all right.
In this day and age of white blood cells and red blood cells,
hematocrit and hemoglobin counts,
bury the mentality that draws blood-red lines in the cool, white sand,
for such divisions lead to death.

Help these speakers of brokenness look for the delicate web of strands drawn from my heart
to you, Merciful God, and
to my special someone, regardless of our sexual orientations,
to the children in our lives, regardless of how they came to be with us, and
to all of creation.

Our family's blood line may end here.
Our family's cosmic eternal line may start here,
With me and this beloved,
With or without children,
Natural or adopted, regardless of their sex or nature.
Thank you for me, just the way I am.

IN PRAISE OF GRANDMOTHERS

Lover of Literature
Singer of Songs
Dancer of Dances

She was medicine to my soul,
A boost to my ego
Honey to my hunger
For knowledge of
Where we came from,
Who we were,
Who I was to become.

Grandmother,
A truly grand mother,
A prayerful woman,
Singing hymns while she washed dishes,
Humming while she swept the floor,
Teaching me our traditions while we ironed.

She nurtured my faith,
Increased my knowledge,
Bandaged my boo-boos,
For the love of God
And of me, child of her child.
I praise God for this
Holy Woman, Wise Woman, Medicine Woman.

IN PRAISE OF ROUGH DIAMONDS

She's a bit of a rough diamond, people say.
Hmm, rough and diamond, the two words make an odd pair.
What does it mean?
How does a rough woman become a diamond or
a jewel of a woman become tough?
From Costa Rica to Scotland to Wyoming, the story's the same.
She works hard for her living and raised kids to boot.
But she'll share her last morsel and give up her bed to someone in need.
To see the sooty roughness fade away, just sit and chat, and
bit by bit, you sink into her plush, warm heart and melt into her clear,
sparkling eyes.
By the time you leave, you both feel cherished; it shows in your face and hers.
The sharp edges of this wizened old dear with the gnarled hands have been sanded to perfection.
Not by a professional jeweler with an eye to the profit margin,
but by the Maker of everything from dust to diamonds.
In her reflection you see yourself;
You get the message.
God loves us rough diamonds, flaws and all.

ON BROKEN RELATIONSHIPS

ON BETRAYAL

Is truth, like beauty, in the eye of the beholder?
Can it be possible that we are both speaking the truth,
but from different sides of the hill?

She said, He said.
One truth gathers in, the other pushes out.
Yet we love the same One.

Like Samuel, I find myself being awakened in the night, confused and dazed.
I don't want to be Jephthah's daughter, sacrificed for someone else's hot-headedness.
No, the Queen of Sheba is more my style.
I like asking hard questions.
I hope for wisdom.

So does truth depend on your perspective?
Maybe so.
The whole truth is we are fragile, broken, human.
Now is the hour for healing and hope.

FOR THOSE CONSIDERING SEPARATION OR DIVORCE

They came over last evening to say goodbye
The wild geese flying in formation.
Slowly, moving in from the southeast,
Honking in the distance to capture my attention,
Then, falling silent as they flew in loose
V's overhead, directly above me.
As they cleared the neighbor's house,
They began honking again, heading
Into the northwest and twilight.
Why did you fall silent overhead?
Did you know that you had my attention?
Was it a silent salute to a kindred spirit,
Or did my wild, high, longing, keening, silent
Heart cry deafen you into silence?

ON SPLITTING THE BLANKET

Boxes of belongings,
The material of a third of a century of life together,
Half packed,
In process.

Some things are easy to pack:
"Her" towel goes; "His" stays behind.
"Her Ladyship's" bathrobe goes; "His Lordship's" remains.
"Her" pillow goes; "His" lies there solitary on the bed.
"Her" books go; "His" books slump in the bookcases.

Other things are harder to pack:
Those things marked "Ours."
The prayer book inscribed to the family from which we read birthday prayers for one another.
Photographs of the family starting with one child, then two,
Infants,
Toddlers,
Children,
Pre-teens,
Teenagers . . .

Soccer pictures,
Picnic pictures,
Party pictures,
Graduation pictures,
Wedding pictures . . .

The latest, of the yet to be born grandchild still in her
pregnant mother's womb . . .

Who gets these: Grandmama? Granddaddy?

When the blanket is split, it's the selvage that's hardest to tear.

FOR TIMES OF WAR

God of Mercy and Justice,
Change comes as surely as
The night becomes day,
Rain falls to the ground,
And buds return in the spring.
Joy comes in the morning (Psalm 30:5).

Comfort is warm.
Security is cozy.
Both flit away as "they" prepare for War.
Wait, take time, listen, and learn.
Violence harms and alarms
    Our hearts and minds, our very souls,
    "This fragile earth, our island home,"
    Time and space itself.
Be still and know that I am God (Psalm 46:10).

When drums beat to the cadence of soldiers marching off to war,
    Wondering becomes the order of the day,
    Waiting is the challenge.
Will her husband be called up?
Their son has already been deployed, their daughter, too.
How about the Mom who's assigned far away from her kids?
And how about the Granddad whose duty was, he thought, already done?
What of the reservists who work all week and then pull two twelve-hour shifts on weekends?
How many mornings will we awake to hear about casualties—theirs and ours?
How many hearts will be broken?
How many families grieving?
And what of Mother Earth?
God will wipe away every tear from their eyes (Revelation 7:17).

We are faced with living in compassionate tension.
Challenge awaits us near and far.
Away—staying human while living through hell.
At home—channeling fear and anxiety into constructive endeavors.
The hands that waved a poster during a peace protest or signed a petition for peace become a sacrament of God's love by reaching out to embrace a friend in need of a different kind of peace.
Then the tension between hawks and doves may be washed away in our communal tears.
They will beat their swords into ploughshares and their spears into pruning hooks (Isaiah 2:4).

May it ever be so. Amen.

ON HEALING

FOR WORRY-WARTS

Merciful God, you know the concerns of my heart, and how I long to bring peace and harmony to those around me. When I am working my way to becoming a "perfect ten" worry-wart, help me to slow down and to breathe deeply. Instead of ranting and raving at everyone and everything around me, remind me to look honestly at the situation. Help me to discern when my opinions or involvement is really needed, and to step back in relief when I am not needed. For I pray in the name of Jesus whose mother and brothers worried about him, too. Amen.

TO WAKE UP THOSE WHO ARE SLEEP-WALKING THROUGH LIFE

Holy One, you who neither slumbers nor sleeps, when we are sleep-walking through life, awaken us to your glorious presence in our lives, in our communities, in our world. Help us balance the excitement of serving you with the human need to have enough rest and sleep for our bodies and minds to function healthfully. For we pray in the name of the Holy Spirit, who re-creates and inspires us. Amen.

FOR THOSE WHO HAVE DIFFICULTY SLEEPING OR RESTING

Jesus, our brother, you experienced both peaceful sleep and the anguish of a sleepless night during your life on earth. When we sleep, let us rest securely in you. When we rest, let us arise refreshed. We lift up those who have trouble sleeping or resting. We ask you to send a spirit of tranquility to them so they may be rejuvenated during their times of rest and sleep. For we pray in the name of the fully human Anointed One of God. Amen.

FOR MEANING AND CONNECTION IN PLACE OF BOREDOM AND LONELINESS

Sacred Three, you show us in your very nature that life and love come through relationships. When we are feeling bored and lifeless, inspire us to take action. When we are feeling lonely, strengthen us to reach out to those around us. Enable us to value all of our relationships—human, animal, plant, and spiritual—so we may flow with the river of life into the ocean of your being. Amen.

FOR PEACE AMIDST THE BUSY-NESS OF LIFE

Spirit, as you moved over the face of the deep, God brought forth all of creation out of a formless void. Move through my being now, so I may become a new creation. May I re-orient my life so instead of busy-ness, I find meaning, and instead of fatigue, I have energy. When the clamoring of good causes becomes overwhelming, help me to center myself in you, so I may be still and know that you are all in all. Amen.

FOR THOSE WHO WAIT

Sit and wait, worry and yawn.
When will the doctors come?
What will the tests show?
Immanuel, God with us between a rock and a hard place.

Sit and wait, stand and stretch.
Day after day, restless nights without end.
We put our dread and our hope in you, O Great Physician of Life.
Uriel, God is my light in the day and in the long hospital nights.

Sit and wait, pace and pray.
Dear God, how the hope and the dread bang against each other.
When, when, when will the answers come?
Gabriel, God is my strength in times of sickness and of wellness.

Stand and praise, jump for joy!
At last the hospital stay's at an end.
The family will be together again,
Heads and hearts pounding their own unique tunes.
Hear the cheers of disbelief and the sighs of glad relief.
Rafael, God heals and reveals . . . Love.

FOR THOSE WITH ADDICTIONS

God of wholeness, we lift up anyone who is or has been addicted to any kind of substance.
For those whose addictions started innocently as a result of a doctor's prescription, have mercy.
For those who wanted to belong so much they paid too high a price, have mercy.
For those who wanted to blot out the intolerable pain of living, have mercy.
And for those who just wanted to have some fun, have mercy.
For those who are not yet in recovery, guide them.
For those who are recovering day by day, strengthen and support them.
For anyone in a relationship with a recovering or active addict, help them to detach lovingly.
For we pray in the name of Jesus, who when faced with a life-or-death struggle, wrestled with it, and then made the hard choice, for the love of God and us, his sisters and brothers. Amen.

FOR THOSE IN NEED OF HEALING THE WOUNDED MODERN MASCULINE OR ETERNAL FEMININE

She sat, spraddle-legged,
in the dusty heat of the August midday
where he had dumped Her,
as he had been once dumped and
as She had been dumped before.

She followed him with moistened eyes
as he drove out of sight.
He drove, without looking in the rear-view mirror,
steeling that oversensitive, tear-filled tenderness
that threatened to bubble up, heat-fired and purgative,
not knowing that She carried with Her
the luminescent alabaster jar
that bore his healing inside.

He disappeared into the heat-miraged distance,
his image already melting
in the waving heat plumes
of the asphalt road.

Holding the jar aloft,
She gracefully arose, her dusty skirts swirling
around her sandaled feet
and walked at right angles to the road
vanishing into the open field of maize
ready for the harvest.

Never mind—
She or one of Her Sisters
would catch up with him
later on down the road.

FOR THOSE FACING DEATH OR MAJOR CHANGES IN LIFE

Life-Giver, this life, the next life, all have beginnings. Just as a tadpole becomes a frog, and a caterpillar changes into a butterfly, so our true selves evolve from one way of being into another.

The snake sloughs off its withered, parched skin to become sleek and slippery, with its wise eyes peering through invisible lids. And the phoenix molders to ashes only to come forth robed in a stunning feathery frock. So our souls, when we die, cast off the sensual thrills and the burdens of pain and limitation these mortal bodies have given. Then they joyfully take on the lithe, gleaming bodies of Resurrection. Draw close to those who are approaching the difficult stages of transformation. We lift them and their loved ones up to you for strength and comfort. Motherly Father, into your hands, we commend our cherished loved ones. We pray in the name of the one who died and arose to new life through the power of the Holy Spirit. Amen.

AT THE SERIOUS ILLNESS OR DEATH OF A PET OR OTHER CREATURE IN YOUR MIDST

Lover of Life, throughout history you have worked through your creatures and the people who love them. We appreciate St. Ephrem's vision of the male animals, fish, and fowl at creation being excited to see the females. We also remember the special gift St. Francis of Assisi had with birds and animals, and St. Clare's love of her cat. In a way pets are sacraments because they provide physical signs of an invisible unconditional love, like yours. Whether the creatures in our lives are pets, work animals, or part of our natural surroundings, give us hearts to see their unique relationships with you. When they are suffering, strengthen us to do what needs to be done to improve their situation. When they are dying, prepare them and us for the new life that lies ahead. Jesus, into your hands, we commend our four-legged, no-legged, winged and finned companions. Amen.

Based on St. Ephrem the Syrian's *Hymns of Virginity 51.1.3–6*

IN HONOR OF PEAR TREES CALLED PEARY AND PERCY

Jesus, you knew the value of pruning and tending fruit trees. Did you feel the anguish of Percy's cut and torn base, and Peary's near-death experience, her trunk whipped and slashed by a careless mower? Thank you for the inspiration to ask for divine healing to complement the sturdy protective collars they now wear. Peary and Percy needed one kind of healing; those who tended them needed another. When Peary burst forth with white blossoms just as Percy broke out in bright green buds, we rejoiced at the realization: God truly loves pear trees and all of creation! The pair of pear trees that had been severely wounded were thriving in the out-pouring of God's Grace. Their two-legged caretakers were healed as memories of violence were replaced by visions of blossoms and buds. Loving Creator, draw near to all parts of your creation that are in distress. Guide the people of Mother Earth to prune carefully when it is needed and to tend respectfully, so all of your Creation may grow in your likeness. Great Spirit, into your hands, we commend our companions of the plant world. Amen.

FOR ROUND PEOPLE IN SQUARE HOLES

FOR CHANGES IN A WOMAN'S MINISTRY (LAY OR ORDAINED)

Gracious God, for so many years, I've cheerfully said, "yes," to family, to church, and to career. My party box is, indeed, full of so many of your gifts. As the needs of my family and work have been fruitful and multiplied, I see the need for some new gifts—time, energy, and the ability to say, "no." I would also appreciate the ability to know in my heart that some "no's" open the way to new and exciting "yeses." While Mary's "yes" to the angel led to intense joy, concern, and grief, with the birth, life, and death of her son, help me see that a prayerfully considered "no" may also lead to joy after working through the initial pain of loss. For I pray in the name of Jesus, the Gift and the Gift-giver. Amen.

FOR CHURCH LEADERS

Good Shepherd, just as the first shepherds of your church discerned the stage of their flock's spiritual development and provided the appropriate nourishment, help the leaders of our local, regional, national, and global churches give milk when they are nurturing spiritual babies, soft food to wee ones, and solid food to mature sisters and brothers in Christ. We ask this so that the shepherds and the sheep of your pasture may grow together in your love through the protection of the Holy Spirit.

BASED ON ST. EPHREM THE SYRIAN'S *SONGS OF NISIBIS 14.16*

TO THE THREE MOST SACRED

I give unto the Father most Glorious, the fears and tears of days gone by,
by crying to Thee this day and always,
I will live in hope and not in doubt.

I give unto the Son most Lowly, the sins of which I'm most ashamed,
by looking on Thee this day and always,
I will not look down, but up and out.

I give unto the Spirit most Holy, the hopes and dreams of years to come,
by trusting in Thee this day and always,
I will live on, and I will sing out.

I give unto Thyself today, my heart, my will, my total self,
by calling on Thee this day and always,
I will go out, and I will come back.

I give unto the Three most Sacred, my life down here and up above,
by hoping in Thee this day and always,
I will sleep in peace and not in fear.

FOR THOSE ASSIMILATING MYSTIC EXPERIENCE

At the point of the fireball blasting into Creation,
Infinite God energy—radiant power—
emerging matter and attracting antimatter,
coupling,
coalescing
congealing
into uncountable myriads of stars,
spiraling far-flung galaxies,
secret, hidden planets
stretching endless throughout God's infinite mind,
God's thoughts forming
from nebulous gas,
from cloudy dust,
from fragmented debris
into orbits and systems,
the glowing and gliding partners
in the awesome, stately dance of the spheres.

At the point of the spear piercing into the side,
finite human pain—guiltless love—
agonizing body and bursting heart,
writhing,
crying,
dying,
into cross-shapen miracles of new life,
descending fiery doves,
quiet, God-given love,
gently spreading throughout human finite frame
new human heart formed
from sins forgiven,
from love known,
from hearts entwined
with the Creator and the Son,
the wounded and risen Lord
of the Sacred Dance of New Creation.

PART FOUR

Mystics, Saints, and Other Extraordinary Folk, Events, and Gifts of Creation

The Mirror

In our dining room, on the wall opposite the china cabinet, there is a mirror. Below it a cookie jar rests tranquilly on top of a silver chest. The mirror shows different aspects of life in a section called "About the Church Calendar." The cookie jar has 364 entries to commemorate all sorts of people, events, and gifts of creation (a.k.a. geomorphology). The silver chest contains prayers, or Collects, for the entries on the calendar marked by a star (*) or number sign (#). May you see the face of the divine in these three sections.

ABOUT THE CHURCH CALENDAR

The churches of the Anglican Communion, as well as the Orthodox and Roman Catholic churches, mark the passing of the days and seasons by observing the church—or liturgical—calendar. Every year, events in the life of Jesus, as well as the lives of Christians throughout the ages, are celebrated on particular days. Here in this chapter is a new liturgical calendar, one that concentrates on little-known Christian women of ages past, both those who gave the world a mighty shove, and those, like Helen Keller, who moved the world as part of an aggregate.[1] Meeting people from ages past involves time travel, a willingness to confront disturbing situations when they arise, and making reality checks to keep our perspective.

For example, we can cheer when a seventh-century woman named Dymphna had the guts to flee her abusive father, even though we're outraged about the reasons for her flight and the violence she suffered when he caught her. And we can be thankful for the people with epilepsy and mental illnesses who were healed by being near Dymphna's tomb, while we ask why her father got away with murder, at least in this life.

A reality check reminds us of two things: the stigma of having epilepsy and mental illness is diminishing, and although incest and abuse are no longer acceptable in many places, there are still women and children and some men who suffer such nightmares. By commemorating Dymphna we remember the people who've fled violent relationships and those who've struggled with epilepsy and mental illnesses. As we aim for healthful relationships, we pay attention to how what we are reading or praying for affects us—intellectually, emotionally, physically, sexually, and spiritually.

Besides people already acknowledged somehow as saints in Christian tradition, I also chose people of other faiths and from recent times because there was something exciting about their lives. Both women and men broke the conventions of their society with great courage, love, and creativity to make their world a better place. Many paid the ultimate price for their convictions. Whether they are single or married, women or men, childless or mothers or fathers of many, the folk on the church, or liturgical, calendar are in some way models for us today, as the prayers following the calendar reveal.

The word *liturgical* comes from Greek words that mean "the work of the people." A liturgical calendar is kind of a list of the many different ways people have been called throughout the ages to work to the glory of God in their communities. Prayers to celebrate the life of a saint or a special event from the Bible and in the Church are called Collects because the significant points about the person or event are collected into a simple prayer. Since the life of someone who has died is usually remembered on the anniversary of the day she or he died, the date on a liturgical, or church, calendar like this is usually the day of death.

However, the people of the world use a variety of calendars, and many cultures are not as focused on dates as our modern western culture is. The people and events on this calendar were chosen because of their interest to women, whether or not the dates of death are known. (Saints and dates were matched as needed.) Often, surprisingly, two wonderful saints died on the same day. Rather than choosing one over the other, duplicate entries were renumbered. When one person was moved to another date because two greats died on the same day, the actual death date is placed in parentheses.

The liturgical calendar includes colors, planets, landforms, iceforms, waterforms, and celestial bodies out of respect for the non-human world and to encourage people to take time to appreciate their surroundings. You may use one of the multi-purpose Collects following the calendar to celebrate these

Gifts of Creation as you come to them on the calendar. Animals, plants, and minerals are not on the calendar because they are given pre-eminence in Part Two. Christmas Day and the Birth of the New Year are the only non-movable events in this calendar.

NOTES

1. Helen Keller, "Humble Tasks," in *The Treasure Chest* (ed. Charles L. Wallis; New York: Harpers & Row, 1965), 240.

The Cookie Jar

THE CHURCH CALENDAR

*The * by an entry means there is a Collect for that entry after the calendar.*
The # by an entry means there is a multi-purpose Collect for that particular Gift of Creation also after the calendar. The Collects for Colors, Planets, Landforms, Iceforms, Waterforms, and Celestial Bodies may be used whenever they are needed.

JANUARY

1 *God's Creation of Humanity, Genesis 1:26
2 *Mary and Felix Barreda, Lay Apostles and Martyrs for Nicaraguan Justice, 1983
3 *St. Seraphim of Sarov, Monk, Mystic, Healer, 1833
4 Mary Mahoney, Pioneer Nurse, 1926
5 George Washington Carver, Educator, Scientist, 1943
6 *God's Revelation (Epiphany) of Jesus, Matthew 2:1–2, 9–12
7 *Kentigerna, Wife, Mother, Homemaker, Widow, Nun, about 733
8 Mary Arthur McElroy, First Lady of U.S.A., 1881–1885, Sister of Chester Arthur, 21st President, 1917
9 Harold Jones (Santee), First Native American Episcopal Bishop of U.S.A., Consecrated 1972
10 (8) *Elizabeth Hooton, Preacher, 1672
11 Students, Teachers, Administrators, Support Staff Beginning a New Term
12 Mev Puelo, Photographer, Witness of Solidarity with Poor, 1996

13 (5) World Environment Day
14 #Shades of the Color Indigo
15 Xu Mu, Poet, Strong Public Leader, Spring and Autumn period, 7th century B.C.E.
16 A Wise Older Woman in Your Heart or Life
17 Barbara Jordan, Orator, Congresswoman, 1996
18 (17) Juliette Gordon Low, "Daisy," Founder of the Girl Guides (Scouts) in U.S.A., 1927
19 Shiphrah and Puah, Midwives, Exodus 1:15–20
20 A Wise Older Man in Your Heart or Life
21 Margaret Dunlop Gibson, Scholar of Semitic Studies, Twin (see 3/22), 1920
22 #The Sun
23 Mary Ward, Inspiration for the Institute of the Blessed Virgin Mary, 1645
24 *Bill W., Co-Founder of Alcoholics Anonymous, 1971
25 *(24) Jeanne Frances de Chantal and Francis de Sales, Founders of the Visitandines, 1641
26 St. Paula, Widow and Scholar, 404
27 (25) Li Tim-Oi, Anglican Priest, China, Ordained 1944
28 *Winter Talk, National Indigenous Peoples Congress (Seminole Nation Episcopal), 1995
29 *(28) Zora Neale Hurston, Pioneer Folklorist, 1960
30 #Deserts
31 St. Marcella, 410, and Elizabeth Ann Bayley Seton, 1821, Widows, Founders of Convents

FEBRUARY

1 The Crew of the Columbia Space Shuttle STS-107, 2003
2 *Mary, Joseph, and Jesus Outside the Temple, Luke 2:21–40
3 (1) *St. Brigid of Ireland, Abbess of First Irish Convent for Women and Men, Bishop, 525
4 Aud "the Deep-Minded," Viking Wise-Woman of Iceland, about 900
5 *Elizabeth Sawyer, Executed as Witch, England, 1621
6 Dorothy, Martyr, Miracle of Roses and Apples, 303
7 Jalal al-Din Rumi, Islamic Mystic, Poet, Founder of Mawlawiy(y)a Sufi Order, 1273 (672 after Hijra)
8 *St. Elfleda, Peacemaker, Co-Abbess of Whitby with her Mother, Eanfleda, 714
9 #Rivers
10 *St. Scholastica, Nun, Perceptive Twin Sister to St. Benedict, 543

11 Mother Meng, Mother of Meng Ke (Mencius), Warring States period, about 350 B.C.E.
12 #Mesas
13 Squaw Chief (Sachem) of the Nipmuc in Massachusetts, 1619
14 Eve, the Mother of All Living
15 Maryam (Mary), Khadija, 619, Fatima, 632, and Asiya, Pharoah's wife, The Four Best Women of Paradise, according to Muhammad
16 Fu Hao, Earliest Female General and Queen Consort, Shang dynasty, 1040 B.C.E.
17 #The Planet Mercury
18 *Sappho, Poet, 570 B.C.E.
19 Ix Chel, Mayan Moon Goddess of Childbirth, Healing, and Weaving
20 #Shades of the Color White
21 *Hagar the Egyptian, the Only Person in the Bible to Call God by Name, Genesis 16 and 21; 25:12
22 Sophie and Hans Scholl, Sister and Brother Leaders of Christian German Resistance to Hitler, Martyrs 1943
23 #Grasslands
24 *Anne B., Co-Founder of Al-Anon Family Group, 1984
25 Felix Varela, Cuban Priest and Patriot of Liberty, 1853
26 (27) Anna Julia Haywood Cooper, Ph.D., Pioneering Scholar, 1964
27 Fred McFeely Rogers, "Mister Rogers," Child Advocate, Good Neighbor, 2003
28 *Martyrs in the Plague of Alexandria, Died Nursing the Sick and Dying, 261

MARCH

1 *Queen of Sheba, 1 Kings 10
2 *Ding Ling, Writer and "Mother" to the New China, 1986
3 Mihri Hatun, Ottoman Poet, 1506
4 Mahadeviyakka, Bhakti (Hindu Devotee) Poet, 12th century
5 Martin Niemoeller, WWI Hero, Lutheran Pastor became Pacifist, 1984
6 Georgia O'Keefe, Artist, 1986
7 Nampeyo, "Snake Woman" (Hopi-Tewa), Potter, Reviver of Early Designs of Traditional Ceramics, 1942
8 #The Planet Venus
9 Victoria Earle Matthews, Founder of the White Rose Mission, 1907
10 *Harriet Tubman, Abolitionist, The Moses of her People, 1913
11 #Shades of the Color Green
12 Founding of the Girl Guides in U.S.A. (predecessor to the Girl Scouts), 1912

13 The Universe as Wisdom Teacher
14 Fannie Lou Hamer, Prophet of Freedom, 1977
15 Sts. Louise de Marillac and Vincent de Paul, Co-founders, the Daughters of Charity, 1660
16 (14) Lucretia Rudolph Garfield, First Lady of U.S.A., 1881, wife of James Garfield, 20th President, 1918
17 (20) Sebastian Castellio, Advocate of Religious Liberty for Catholics and Calvinists, Lyons and Geneva, 1563
18 #Bays
19 *St. Joseph of Nazareth, Jesus' Father Figure
20 (21) *International Day of Women and the Vernal Equinox
21 International Day for the Elimination of Racial Discrimination, U.N., 1960
22 (23) Agnes Smith Lewis, Scholar of Semitic Studies, Twin (see 1/21), 1926
23 Army Pfc. Lori Ann Piestewa, Hopi, Killed in Combat, Iraq, 2003
24 *Archbishop Oscar Romero, Martyr of San Salvador, 1980
25 *Mary Joyfully Accepts Becoming Jesus' Mother (The Annunciation), Luke 1:46–55
26 (24) *Wanda Lee, Spiritual Gifts of Divination and Encouragement in her Craft Community, 1993
27 (25) Ida B. Wells-Barnett, Teacher, Journalist, Crusader for Justice, 1931
28 (30) *Abigail Powers Fillmore, Teacher, First Lady of U.S.A., 1850–1853, Wife of Millard Fillmore, 13th President, 1853
29 (30) Ellen Swallow Richards, Chemist, Pioneer in Sanitary Engineering and Human Ecology, 1911
30 Sister Thea Bowman, African-American Franciscan, 1990
31 Mother Maria Skobtsova, Orthodox Nun and Martyr, 1945

APRIL

1 #Shades of the Color Yellow
2 *The Syro-Phoenician or Cannonite Woman, Matthew 9:20–21; Mark 7:25; Luke 8:43–48
3 #Tundra
4 "The Divine" Sarah Vaughn, A Musician's Singer, 1990
5 *Pandita Ramabai, "Mother of Modern India," Indian Christian Advocate of Women and Poor, Valued Indian Culture, 1922
6 Hadewijch of Brabant, Beguine Mystic, 13th century
7 Irene McCoy Gaines, Civil Rights Reformer, 1964
8 Marian Anderson, Classical Music Pioneer, 1993
9 *Sacajawea, Guide with the Lewis and Clark Expedition, 1884

10 (7) André Trocmé, a Righteous Gentile, 1971
11 *Rabi'a al-'Adawiyya of Iraq, Sufi (Islamic) Mystic, 801 (185 after Hijra)
12 Priscilla and Aquila, Tentmakers, Evangelists, Church Administrators, Martyrs, Acts of the Apostles, 18, 64
13 #Highlands
14 *Rachel Carson, Mother of the Modern Environmental Movement, 1964
15 #The Planet Earth and Its Moon
16 *Mirra Loxvickaja, Poet, about 1904
17 *Blessed Kateri Tekakwitha, the Lily of the Mohawks, 1680
18 *Martha, A Persian Martyr, about 341
19 Deborah, Judge of Israel, Judges 4–5
20 St. Agnes Da Montepulciano, Healer, Mystic, Visions of Baby Jesus, 1317
21 *Lu Meiniang, Craftswoman, Parasol Designer and Maker, Tang dynasty, about 791
22 Kathe Kollwitz, Pacifist, Artist, 1945
23 *Margaret Fell Fox, Organizational and Pastoral Care Leader of the Quakers, 1702
24 Willa Cather, Teacher, Writer, Journalist, Critic, 1947
25 #Glaciers
26 Gaia, Mother Goddess of Earth and the Soul
27 Dong Bai, Courtesan and Poet, Held to her Principles, Ming and Qing dynasties, 1651
28 *Amos, Prophet, Advocate for Social Justice, 8th century B.C.E.
29 Catherine of Sienna, Mystic, Social Activist, 1380
30 A Child in Your Heart or Life

MAY

1 May Day
2 (1) Edmonia "Wildfire" Lewis, Sculptress, died circa 1911
3 *The Woman with a Flow of Blood, Matthew 9:20–22; Mark 5:25–34; Luke 8:43–48
4 *Monica, Mother of Augustine of Hippo, 387
5 Tarbula, Persian Martyr, about 342
6 Blessed Angela of Foligno, Mystic, Widow, Theologian, Third Order Franciscan, 1309
7 #Woodlands
8 *Dame Julian of Norwich, Mystic, about 1417
9 Madame Lu, Advocate for Justice, Order and Virtue, Western Han dynasty, 17

10 #Icebergs

11 Huldah, Prophetess, 2 Kings 22:14; 2 Chronicles 34:22

12 Students, Teachers, Administrators, Support Staff Preparing for Finals, Graduation

13 Emma Azalia Smith Hackley, Musician, Educator, Activist, Philanthropist, 1922

14 Emily Dickinson, Poet, Lover of Nature, 1886

15 Gloria Anzaldua, Lesbian Chicana Poet, Writer, 2004

16 *Dymphna, Patron of Epileptics and the Mentally Ill, about 650

17 Blessed Josephine Bakhita of Sudan, Ex-Slave and Nun, 1947

18 Mary McLeod Bethune, Educator, Activist, U.S. Government Official, 1955

19 A Young Woman You Appreciate

20 #The Planet Mars

21 Xie Daoyun, Poet, Eastern Jin dynasty, born about 376

22 *Martha Dandridge Custis Washington, First Lady of U.S.A., 1789–1797, Wife of George Washington, 1st President, 1802

23 Euphrosyne of Polotsk, Russia, Scribe, Pilgrim, Gave to Poor, 1173

24 *Bilhah, Genesis 30:6, Zilpah, Genesis 30:11, and All Surrogate Mothers

25 *Wang Zhenyi, Scientist, Qing dynasty, 1797

26 Woman of Endor, Seer, 1 Samuel 28:7–25

27 #Shades of the Color Orange

28 #Savannahs

29 *The Visitation of Mary to Elizabeth, Luke 1:35–56

30 Joan of Arc, Visionary, Advisor to King, Military Leader, 1431

31 *Those Who Have Experienced Armed Conflict

JUNE

1 Marguerite Porete, Beguine Preacher, Mystic, Martyr, 1310

2 Anthony de Mello, Priest and Spiritual Guide, 1987

3 A Young Man You Appreciate

4 *Jephthah's Daughter, Judges 11:34–40, A Woman Christ-figure (Her Death Foreshadowed Christ's Death)

5 Mary Ann Shadd Cary, Pioneer Journalist, Lecturer, 1893

6 The Sphinx, Egyptian Goddess of Birth, Death, and Wisdom

7 Seattle, Chief of the Suquamish, 1866

8 Emily Tubman, Early Leader in the Disciples of Christ, 1885

9 *St. Columba, Abbot of Iona, Unofficial Patron of Abused Women and Girls, 597, and *St. Ephrem the Syrian, Deacon, Hymn-writer for Women's Choirs, 373

10 *Founding of the Society of Alcoholics Anonymous, 1935
11 #Fjords
12 The Widow of Zarephath, 1 Kings 17:8–24; Luke 4:25–26
13 Martin Buber, Jewish Philosopher, 1965
14 Peacemakers
15 Ella Fitzgerald, First Lady of Jazz, 1996
16 The Unmarried Woman, 1 Corinthians 7:34
17 *Susanna Wesley, The Moral and Religious Mother of Methodism, 1742, and Evelyn Underhill, Mystic, Married London Homemaker, 1941
18 #The Planet Jupiter
19 #Canyons
20 Blessed Osanna Andreasi, Mystic, Spiritual Advisor, 1505
21 *Summer Solstice
22 *Female Slave of Phillipi, Acts 16:16
23 *Betty Shabazz, Model of Perseverance, College Official, Civil Rights Leader, 1997
24 Mary Church Terrell, Advocate for Equality, 1954
25 *Sadhu Sundar Singh, Teacher, Evangelist, and Indian Mystic, 1929
26 #Shades of the Color Gold
27 *Helen Keller, Author, Blind, Deaf, Advocate for the Blind and Handicapped, 1880
28 Phebe, Deaconess at Cenchrea, Romans 16:1–2
29 #Swamps
30 Li Yin, Poet, Painter, Intellectual, Ming and Qing dynasties, about 1685

JULY

1 Dr. Bhimrao Ramji Ambedkar, Foremost Human Rights Activist in India, 1956
2 St. Thomas the Apostle
3 *Enmegahbowh "One-who-stands-before-his-people," (Ojibwa-Ottawa), Methodist Preacher, First Native American Episcopal Priest, 1902
4 Elizabeth of Portugal, Peacemaker, Builder of Hospitals, Orphanages, Convents, 1336
5 (3) Harriet Lane, First Lady of U.S.A., 1857–1861, Niece of James Buchanan, 15th President, 1903
6 #Shades of the Color Red
7 *Fethullah Gulen, Teacher, Humanitarian, Muslim Cleric, born 1938
8 Belteshazzar's Mother, Wise Queen Mother of Babylonia, Daniel 5:10–12
9 Rose Hawthorne, Founder of Servants of Relief for Incurable Cancer, N.Y., 1926
10 #Oceans

11 A Teenager or Young Person in Your Heart or Life
12 Veronica, Cared for Jesus on the way to his Crucifixion, 1st century
13 Frida Kahlo, Artist, 1954
14 Mayoca, Fyndoca, Fincana MacDonald and their Sisters, Missionaries in Scotland, 8th century
15 Our Common Mother, Transmitter of Mitochondrial DNA Present in Every Modern Human, Lived between 140,000–290,000 years ago
16 May Sarton, Poet, Writer, Lesbian, 1995
17 Nairobi Forward-Looking Strategies for the Advancement of Women, U.N. World Conference, July 1985 (Endorsed by the U.N. General Assembly, December 1985)
18 (19) St. Macrina the Younger, with her Widowed Mother, Founders of One of the First Convents, 379
19 *First Convention for Women's Rights, Declaration of Rights and Sentiments Adopted, Seneca Falls, N.Y., 1848, and Beginning of the Women's Rights Movement in U.S.A., 1848
20 #Rainbows
21 *Sun Bu-Er, Mother of Three, Taoist Sage, about 1124
22 *St. Mary Magdalene, Apostle and Preacher, Matthew 27:56, 61; 28:1; Mark 15:41, 47; 16:1, 9; Luke 8:2; 24:10; John 19:25; 20:1, 11, 16, 18
23 Divine Messengers
24 #Hills
25 Susanna, Generous Evangelist, Luke 8:3
26 Blessed Bartholomea Capitanio, Founder of Sisters of Charity, for a Girls' School, Providing Nurses, 1833
27 *St. Mechtild of Magdeburg, Mystic, Prophet, about 1282
28 *Martha of Bethany, Evangelist, and Her Sister, Mary, John 11:17–44
29 (28) Charlotte Gulick, 1938, and Luther Gulick, 1918, Co-Founders of Camp Fire Girls (now Camp Fire U.S.A.), 1910
30 #Deltas
31 #The Planet Saturn

AUGUST

1 *Lady Song, Three Kingdoms period, Scholar, 364
2 *Um Kolthom, Egyptian Singer, 1975
3 #Shades of the Color Blue
4 Students, Teachers, Administrators, Support Staff Beginning for a New Term
5 "Mother Ann" Lee, Founder of the Shakers, 1784

6 *The Transfiguration of the Beloved Son, Matthew 17:1–8; Mark 9:2–8; Luke 9:28–36
7 (6) Ellen Wilson, Painter, First Lady of U.S.A., 1913–1914, 1st Wife of Woodrow Wilson, 28th President, 1914
8 Kassiane, Byzantine Greek Poet, circa 843
9 Tlazolteotl, Toltec Earth Mother Goddess of Love, Desire, and Forgiveness
10 Mãe Menininha do Gantois (a.k.a Maria Escolástica da Conceição Nazaré), Revered Priestess of Brazil's African-based Candomblé Religion, 1986
11 *St. Clare, Abbess at Assisi, Founder of the Poor Clares, 1253, and *St. Mary, the Mother of Jesus, Luke 1:26–56, 2:1–7, 16–19
12 Someone You Can Laugh With
13 Florence Nightingale, Nurse, Social Reformer, 1910
14 Athanasia, Widow, Nun, Adviser to Empress Theodora, about 860
15 (18) Anne Hutchison, First Woman Preacher in New World, Puritan Prophet, 1643
16 Mirabai, Hindu Poet-Saint, 1565
17 Pearl Bailey, Ambassador of Love, Entertainer, Author, 1990
18 Ratification of the 19th Amendment to the Constitution, Women's Right to Vote, 1920
19 Burgundofara, 657, and Blessed Emily Bicchieri, 1314, Abbesses of Convents
20 *Bernard of Clairvaux, Abbot, Poet, Hebraist in France, 1153
21 Liang Hongyu, Strategist, General and National Heroine, Northern and Southern Song dynasties, 1135
22 #The Planet Uranus
23 Rose of Lima, Mystic, 1617
24 Elisabeth Kübler-Ross, Pioneer on Humanizing Death and Dying, 2004
25 Simone Weil, Philosopher and Mystic, 1948
26 Someone You Can Sob With
27 Bishop Dom Helder Camara, Brazilian Advocate of Peace and Justice, born 1909
28 Wise Woman of Tekoa, 2 Samuel 14:1–20
29 Bathildis, Slave, Queen of Franks, Regent, Ransomed Captives, Nun, 680
30 #Moors
31 *Aidan, Bishop of Lindisfarne, England, Patron of Arts, Mentor to Abbesses, 651

SEPTEMBER

1 *David Pendleton Oakerhater (a.k.a. Oakenhater, "*O-kuh-ha-tuh*") "Making Medicine" (Cheyenne), 1931
2 Eulalia Perez, Lemonade Maker and Exporter, 1877
3 Ban Zhao, Historian, Mathematician and Astronomer, Eastern Han dynasty, 120
4 Tanaka Shozo, Japan's Pioneer Conservationist, 1913
5 *The Pankhurst Family: Mother, Emmeline, 1928, and Father, Richard, 1898, and their Daughters, Christabel, 1958, Sylvia, 1960, and Adela, 1961, Militant Women's Rights Advocates
6 *Bega, Founder of St. Bee's Monastery, Gave to the Poor and Oppressed, 7th century
7 Sarah Garnet, Educator, Suffragist, 1911
8 Sarah Mapps Douglass, Educator, Abolitionist, 1882, and Frederick Douglass, Abolitionist, Women's Rights Orator, 1895
9 *Sidqi of Turkey, Sufi Poet, Mystic, Celibate, 1703
10 *Blessed Teresa of Calcutta, Founder of the Missionaries of Charity, 1997
11 *9/11/01
12 A Girl in Your Heart or Life
13 #Caverns
14 A Boy in Your Heart or Life
15 *Feng Liao, Diplomat and Ambassador for Han dynasty, 50 B.C.E.
16 Hallie Q. Brown, Educator, Activist, Author, 1949
17 Hildegarde of Bingen, Mystic, Nun, 1179
18 *Dag Hammarskjold, Secretary General of the U.N., 1961
19 Ni Kwei-tseng Soong, Mother of Methodism in China, 1931
20 Lydia Cabrera, Writer, Anthropologist, Advocate of Afro-Cuban Culture, 1991
21 Lord Serphant of the Family of Serpent Stone (Wil Martin), Craft Elder, 1996
22 Alice Hamilton, Pathologist in Industrial Diseases, 1970
23 *Autumnal Equinox
24 Margery Kempe, Mystic, Pilgrim, about 1438
25 (22) Sor Juana Ines de la Cruz of New Spain (Mexico), Nun, Poet, Scientist, 1695
26 Adamnan, Hagiographer, Abbot of Iona, Protector of Women and Children, 704
27 #Lakes
28 #The Planet Neptune
29 *St. Michael and All Angels, Daniel 10
30 #Shades of the Color Brown

OCTOBER

1 *National Breast Cancer Awareness Month
2 (1) Maria Mitchell, Astronomer, Discovered a Comet, 1847
3 *Agneta Chang, a Maryknoll Sister, Founder of the Sisters of Our Lady of Perpetual Help in North Korea, Martyr, 1950
4 *St. Francis of Assisi, Friar, Founder of the Franciscans, 1226
5 *Lois W., Co-Founder of Al-Anon Family Group, 1988
6 Daisy Elizabeth Adams Lampkin, Social Reformer, Fund-Raiser, 1964
7 *Rubye Doris Smith Robinson, Leader of the Student Non-Violent Coordinating Committee, 1967
8 St. Bridget of Sweden, Mother of 8, Mystic, Founder of the Most Holy Trinity, "Brigettines," 1373
9 *Anna Freud, Pioneer Child Psychologist, 1982, and *National Depression Screening Day
10 Shirin Ebadi, Iranian Judge, Human Rights Advocate, Nobel Peace Prize Winner, born 1947 .
11 Sister Ignatia Gavin, Founder of Rosary Hall, Rehabilitation of Alcoholics, 1952 (see 11/16, Dr. Bob)
12 (11) National Coming Out Day, begun 1987
13 (5) Catherine Booth, "Mother" of the Salvation Army, 1890
14 (16) Flora Nwapa, Teacher, Author, Nigerian Government Official, Businesswoman, Publisher, 1993
15 St. Teresa of Avila, Mystic, Strongly Independent Woman, 1582
16 *Sarah Winnemucca Hopkins, Interpreter, Teacher, Advocate for Native American Rights, 1891
17 National Mammography Day for National Breast Cancer Awareness Month
18 *St. Luke the Evangelist, Luke 1–2
19 #Forests
20 'A'isha bint Abi Bakr, Source of 1,210 Hadith (Traditions about Muhammad), 670 (50 after Hijra)
21 #The Planet Pluto
22 Maura O'Halloran, Christian Zen Monk, 1982
23 Lucy Craft Laney, School Founder, 1933
24 (23) *St. James the Just of Jerusalem, Jesus' Brother, Martyr, about 62, Galatians 1:19
25 Kaltes, Ugric (Siberian) Moon Goddess of Fertility and Rejuvenation
26 *Women's Rights Advocates Elizabeth Cady Stanton, Biblical Scholar, Writer, 1902, and Susan B. Anthony, Orator, 1906
27 (28) *In Commemoration of Anna the Prophet and Evangelist and Simeon the Priest, Luke 2:36–38

28 Abigail Adams, Women's Rights Advocate, First Lady of U.S.A., 1797–1801, Wife of John Adams, 2nd President, 1818
29 #Shades of the Color Black
30 Madame Gong Sun, Fencing-Dancer, Tang dynasty, 756
31 All Hallows Eve

NOVEMBER

1 All Saints
2 *Commemoration of the Day of the Dead
3 #Mountains
4 *Raissa Maritain, Poet and Contemplative, 1960
5 Anna Louise Strong, American Journalist in China, Advocate for Justice, 1970
6 May Swenson, Poet, Observer of Nature, 1989
7 Anna Eleanor Roosevelt, Diplomat, Humanitarian, First Lady of U.S.A., 1933–1945, Wife of F. D. Roosevelt, 1962
8 *Maria Petrovykh (1979), Mother, Poet, Editor, Translator, and her daughter, Arisha Golovacheva
9 #Shades of the Color Violet
10 (15) St. Elizabeth of Hungary, Mother, Charitable Works, 1231
11 (12) Gertrude the Great, Mystic, Author, 1302
12 Wilma Rudolph, Olympic Sprinter, 1994
13 (14) Meridel Le Sueur, Advocate for Farm and Factory Workers, Native Peoples, Women, and the Earth, 1996
14 Consecration of Samuel Seabury in Aberdeen, Scotland as the first Episcopal Bishop of U.S., Birth of the Anglican Communion, 1784
15 Margaret Mead, Anthropologist, 1978
16 *Dr. Bob, Co-Founder of Alcoholics Anonymous, 1950
17 *Audre Lorde, Black, Lesbian, Mother, Warrior Poet, 1992
18 *St. Hilda, Abbess of Whitby, 680
19 *Lois Clark (Creek), Teacher, Author, Instrumental in Establishing Saint's Day for David Oakerhater (a.k.a. Oakenhater), 1985
20 (16) *St. Margaret, Queen of Scotland, Mother, Advocate for Social Justice, 1093
21 Zhuo Wenjun, Poet, Western Han dynasty, 118 B.C.E.
22 World Children's Day
23 A Woman in the Autumn of her Life
24 #Stars and Their Systems
25 St. Catherine of Alexandria, Patron of Philosophers, Maidens, and Preachers, Martyr, about 310
26 *Sojourner Truth, Evangelist, Abolitionist, Women's Rights Orator, 1883

27 Thanksgiving Day (Changeable Date)
28 A Man in the Autumn of his Life
29 Dorothy Day, Founder of "The Catholic Worker" movement, 1980
30 Etty Hillesum, Mystic of the Holocaust, 1943

DECEMBER

1 *Rosa Parks, One of the Sparks of the Civil Rights Movement in 1955, Montgomery, Alabama, 2003
2 Jean Donovan, Maura Clarke, M.M., Sr. Ita Ford, M.M., Sr. Dorothy Kazel, O.S.U., Martyrs of El Salvador, 1980
3 Mary Baker Eddy, Founder of the Church of Christ, Scientist, 1910
4 Students, Teachers, Administrators, Support Staff Preparing for Finals, Graduation
5 *Phillis Wheatley, Published Poet, Founder of African-American Literature, 1784
6 Asella, 12-year-old Recluse, Visited by Bishop, Historian, Praised by Jerome, 406
7 *Rosie the Riveter, 1940s
8 Golda Meir, Third Prime Minister of Israel, 1978
9 Theris (Buddhist Nuns) of China, circa 80 B.C.E.
10 The Woman of Bethany Who Anointed Jesus, Luke 7:36–50
11 Sister Alicia Domon and Mothers of the Disappeared of Argentina, 1977
12 *Our Lady of Guadalupe
13 #Volcanoes
14 Hina, Polynesian Creator of All and Moon Goddess
15 Maggie L. Walker, Bank President, Pioneered Economic Independence among African-American Women, 1934
16 Vashti, Queen of Persia, Esther 1
17 The Shunammite Woman, 2 Kings 4:8–37; 8:1–6
18 *U.N. Convention of the Elimination of all Forms of Discrimination against Women, 1979
19 Pretty Shield, Crow Medicine Woman, 1938
20 #The Life/Energy Beyond our Senses
21 *Winter Solstice
22 A Baby in Your Heart/Mind
23 *Rabbi Abraham Heschel, Asked God for and Received Wonder, not Success, in Life, 1972
24 John Muir, Naturalist, Writer, Conservationist, Founder of the Sierra Club, 1914

25 *Celebration of Jesus' Birth
26 #Shades of the Color Silver
27 #Prairies
28 Edith Wilson, First Lady of U.S.A., 1915–1921, Wilson's Unofficial Chief of Staff, 2nd Wife of Woodrow Wilson, 28th President, 1961
29 *St. Melania the Younger, Philanthropist, Founder of Churches, Convents, Monasteries, Pilgrim, 439
30 *Josephine Butler, Worker among Women, 1905
31 *Birth of the New Year

The Silver Chest

COLLECTS

Here are the Collects for over a hundred entries from the church calendar. These prayers commemorate people of various faiths and places, events of special significance to us as women, and others that are vital to us as human beings.

Since the Gifts of Creation have been sprinkled throughout the calendar, these multi-purpose Collects for Colors, Planets, Landforms, Iceforms, Waterforms, and Celestial Bodies may be used whenever they are needed.

COLLECT FOR COLORS

GRACIOUS GOD, you chose a rainbow as a sign of hope for the future of humanity and life on Earth. We praise you for the way the atmosphere during or after rain works together to create something as beautiful and bright as a rainbow. Thank you for the reds, oranges, yellows, greens, blues, indigoes, and violets of the arcs of color across the sky. We also appreciate the other colors of nature, the browns, blacks, whites, silvers, and golds. Like the colors all around us, may we reflect some small measure of the breadth of your Grace to others. Amen.

COLLECT FOR PLANETS

HOLY CREATOR, we praise you for Mercury, Venus, Earth, Mars, Jupiter, Saturn, Uranus, Neptune, and Pluto. We also thank you for the role the planets in our universe have in influencing our lives here on Earth. We appreciate their stability and the orbits, moons, rings, and other features that make each planet unique. Thank you for the way the planets and the universe demonstrate your majesty. May we follow their examples of being parts of a magnificent whole. Amen.

COLLECT FOR LANDFORMS

LIFE-GIVER, we praise you for the many different kinds of landforms there are on the Earth. Mother Earth has such a variety of features from the heights of Mt. Everest to the depths of the Grand Canyon and so much in between. We appreciate the landforms themselves and the life that each sustains, from the water lilies and alligators of the swamps, to the frogs of the fens, to the cacti and snakes of the mesas, deserts, and dry places. Whether the form is high or low, flat or round and craggy, whether it's near water and wooded or in a dry, barren place, all add to the health of the planet's ecosystems. Guide us in being better partners with the landforms that share the Earth with us. Amen.

COLLECT FOR ICEFORMS

O YE MAKER OF FROST AND COLD, of glaciers and icebergs, we praise you for the barrenness and beauty of the iceforms, and also for the walruses, polar bears, and other amazing creatures of the frozen lands and icy waters. Thank you for the vital roles the iceforms play in the cycle of life, death, and new life. We appreciate what the iceforms and their denizens teach us about living on Mother Earth. Amen.

COLLECT FOR WATERFORMS

JESUS, you were baptized in the Jordan River as a sign of repentance and of birth into new life. We praise you for the many waterforms on the Earth. We treasure the life that lives in the salt water of the oceans and the fresh water of tiny creeks, huge rivers and waterways, and lakes. We thank you that there are bodies of fresh water large enough to give refuge to unknown creatures of the deep and wee lochs that come from rain filling a depression in the land. May we treat the waterforms of this Earth with respect, so they and all manner of life dependent on them are able to thrive. Amen.

COLLECT FOR CELESTIAL BODIES

HEAVENLY MOTHER-FATHER, we praise you for the sun and moon, and the stars and their systems. Thank you for the light and warmth the sun gives and for the way the moon reflects that light to us. We thank you for the stars and their gifts of light, guidance in navigation, and sheer inspiration. We also recognize and appreciate the Life/Energy that is beyond our human sense of perception. May we be sensitive to the forces around us, even those that are far above us in the sky. Amen.

January 1

God's Creation of Humanity, **Genesis 1:26**

GOD OF GOODNESS AND WHOLENESS, we recall that in the beginning when you created the first humans, you gave the care of their environment to both sexes. We rejoice with you in the inherent goodness of your creation, and we praise you for creating us, male and female, in your image. Forgive us for overlooking the divine image in each person and for our part in hurting the ecosystems of our world. Help us, we pray, to see all of creation as you do so we may be nurturing caretakers of all you have created. For we pray as we hope, in the power of the Holy Spirit. Amen.

January 2

Mary and Felix Barreda, **Lay Apostles and Martyrs for Nicaraguan Justice, 1983**

MOTHERLY FATHER, we praise you for your servant leaders Mary and Felix and the love they experienced through the Cursillo Movement. We thank you for their courage in putting their faith into action by caring for the poor of Nicaragua. Even though their choice meant risking their lives because of the political climate, they chose to work joyfully and diligently to harvest the coffee crop in exchange for necessities for those in need. We recall with outrage the brutality Felix and, especially, Mary suffered when the Contras kidnapped them. We extol Mary and Felix for holding fast to their faith, instead of denouncing it in favor of communism. We acknowledge that few, if any of us, will ever be in such life-threatening situations. Yet we ask for help in putting our faith into action so pervasively that we may truly change society for the good of all. For we pray in the name of Jesus, the Servant King. Amen.

January 3

St. Seraphim of Sarov, **Monk, Mystic, Healer, 1833**

HOLY GOD OF INNER VISION, we praise you for calling Seraphim into your service as a monk, mystic, and healer. We especially remember him for instructing the rich man he healed to give away his riches, free his serfs, and live in poverty. Thank you for working through this simple Russian monk to give his society and ours an example of how those with money and power are to deal with the weaker, less fortunate members of society. For it is in the name of Jesus, the son of a carpenter who was born in a stable, we pray. Amen.

January 6

God's Revelation (Epiphany) of Jesus, Matthew 2:1–2, 9–12

ALL-KNOWING AND UNSPEAKABLE GOD, we praise you for revealing your son to the holy men of the East. Thank you for affirming the inherent goodness of human birth, and of knowledge and wisdom. In calling the magi from the East to Bethlehem, we learn that anyone looking for you can find you, regardless of their circumstances. We pray to you, O God, who brought this world into being, in the name of the Baby who was made known on this day, and in the power of the Holy Spirit who calls us into union with the Holy Three. Amen.

January 7

Kentigerna, Wife, Mother, Homemaker, Widow, Nun, about 733

HOLY GOD, we praise you for your servant Kentigerna and for her experiences as a wife, mother, and homemaker that she brought to her ministry as a nun. We thank you that she had the gifts to minister to those in her midst, and that she was also willing to devote the last years of her life solely to you, as a solitary on a bleak Scottish island. Whether we are called to minister in the thick of our families and communities or to draw away to some secluded spot, help us to serve you in love and joy. For we pray in the name of Jesus who valued his solitude and his community, the world. Amen.

January 10 (8)

Elizabeth Hooton, Preacher, 1672

DIVINE LIGHT, we praise you for this woman who was the first convert to Quakerism and went on to become the first Quaker woman minister. We recall Elizabeth's faithful witness to you and her boldness in speaking out to the powerful men in her society. Her continued preaching was especially courageous because she suffered repeated imprisonment and physical hardship that eventually led to her death. We lament the conditions that led to the religious persecution of Quakers and bold women like Elizabeth. Empower us to work for religious freedom and the dignity of each individual. For we pray in the name of the Light of the world. Amen.

January 24

Bill W., Co-Founder of Alcoholics Anonymous, 1971

LOVING GOD, we praise you for your son, Bill, and for his friendship with Dr. Bob. We are especially thankful for their founding of Alcoholics Anonymous as a support group for people struggling with alcoholism. We are relieved that alcoholism is becoming more fully understood as a disease rather than a character flaw. Attending A.A. meetings and being involved in the program as it has developed through the years has improved the lives of countless people. We lift up anyone who has experienced the suffering and desperation of being or loving an alcoholic. May they find the serenity that being a part of A.A. or Al-Anon Family Groups offers. Amen.

January 25 (24)

Jeanne Frances de Chantal and Francis de Sales, Founders of the Visitandines, 1641

SACRED THREE, we praise you for calling Jeanne into partnership with Francis to establish the Congregation of the Visitation. We appreciate Francis's vision of a place for girls and widows to lead a religious life without the austerity of other orders. We celebrate the leadership abilities Jeanne developed as a wife and mother because they later enabled her to be an effective abbess. Although some may question Jeanne's decision to start the Visitandines when she still had children at home, we thank you that she had the means and the time to make provisions for them. When we are at the crossroads of life, send us trustworthy people to support us in our decisions and help us to take the time to discern your will before we leap into action. For we pray in the name of the One-in-Three and Three-in-One. Amen.

January 28

Winter Talk, National Indigenous Peoples Congress (Seminole Nation Episcopal), 1995

GREAT HOLY SPIRIT, we praise you for drawing the indigenous peoples of the Episcopal Church to this Winter Talk and for their work in drawing up their Statement of Self-Determination. We celebrate their declaration of themselves as free and equal members of the Episcopal Church and the Anglican Communion. We rejoice with them in proclaiming the value of their ancient heritage and great traditions. We respect them as survivors of a tragic history. We are thankful for their willingness to forgive and to welcome others to work with them in justice, faith, and compassion. Just as these sisters and brothers have blended their traditions and customs into their celebration of the Gospel, help us to claim the life-giving parts of our various heritages and to be open to people of other faiths. In the name of the God of Justice and Mercy, we pray. Amen.

January 29 (28)

Zora Neale Hurston, **Pioneer Folklorist, 1960**

MERCIFUL GOD OF JUSTICE, we praise you for your daughter Zora, and the strong sense of independence she gained from growing up in an all-black, self-governing town. We also thank you for Zora's work collecting and publishing African-American and African-Caribbean folklore. Her literary creativity and folklore-inspired writing have greatly influenced American black culture. When life's circumstances require freedom of thought, remind us of Zora's life-long independence. Amen.

February 2

Mary, Joseph, and Jesus Outside the Temple, **Luke 2:21–40**

HOLY GOD, at the appropriate time Mary, the Mother of our Lord, and Joseph brought Jesus to the temple for purification according to the traditions of their religion. We praise you for sending your only begotten son to be carried and given birth to by a woman, just as we carry and deliver our babies. We especially thank you for showing us that a mother and baby need not be purified to be worthy of your gifts. We recall that Simeon showered his prophecy on Baby Jesus and Mary before either was ritually purified. We claim the innate goodness of our girl and boy babies and of ourselves before, during, and after childbirth. It is exciting to see that, in Simeon's response to the new baby, men can enjoy baby showers as much as women do! Amen.

February 3 (1)

St. Brigid of Ireland, **Abbess of First Irish Convent for Women and Men, Ordained Bishop, 525**

SACRED THREE, we praise you for the authority and charisma you gave Brigid and for her place as one of the three patron saints of Ireland. We affirm her decision to invite a bishop to join her community and to share her leadership. We especially applaud the perception Brigid showed in choosing a bishop who was willing to go beyond the conventional limits of the sexes by consecrating her to be a bishop. We mourn the centuries of disbelief and excuses that have turned an exciting movement of the Holy Spirit into mere mythology. Help us to proclaim your work in our lives no matter how unconventional it may be. For it is in the name of the Mother-Father, and of the Son, and of the Holy Spirit we pray. Amen.

February 5

***Elizabeth Sawyer,* Executed as Witch, England, 1621**

MERCIFUL GOD, we praise you for your daughter, Elizabeth, and for all of the women and men who were executed as witches or wizards during the Burning Times. We ask for healing for the spiritual damage done by religious officials who advocated persecution, humiliation, psychological trauma, and execution. We lift up those who were accused simply because they were different. We thank you for working through people with gifts of healing and spiritual insight, regardless of the precise tenets of their personal faith. Open our eyes to see you wherever you are. For we pray in the name of the Crucified and Risen One. Amen.

February 8

***St. Elfleda,* Peacemaker, Co-Abbess of Whitby with her mother, Eanfleda, 714**

MOTHERLY FATHER, we praise you for this remarkable mother-daughter team who succeeded the great St. Hilda as abbesses of Whitby. We celebrate Elfleda's gifts as a peacemaker and as a church leader. We especially appreciate Elfleda and Eanfleda's willingness to share the responsibilities of running the convent. When we are tempted to take excessive responsibility or to try to go it alone, remind us of the joy these two women found in working together. Regardless of our ages and abilities, help us to value those older and younger than we are so that your love may be fully experienced across the generations in our communities. For we pray we in the name of the Messiah who came into this world as a baby and grew to maturity. Amen.

February 10

***St. Scholastica,* Nun, Perceptive Twin Sister to St. Benedict, 543**

MOTHERLY FATHER, we praise you for Scholastica's great love of you, and for your affirmation of her love for her brother Benedict. We recall that, near the end of her life, when Scholastica wanted to spend more time with him, he refused for the sake of his monastery's rules. We celebrate the thunderstorm you sent in answer to Scholastica's prayer and we thank you for listening to her when her own twin brother would not. Open our ears and our hearts that we may truly hear what's being asked of us so our families and community may feel your love through us. Amen.

February 18

Sappho, Poet, 570 B.C.E.

HOLY LOVE, we praise you for Sappho's creativity and the great love she put into her poems. Although she lived at a time that was hostile to women's gifts and was orphaned at an early age, she was independent enough to write what she really felt. We also thank you that at least some of her poems survived. Inspire us to be honest with our feelings and to value women and their gifts, all of them. For we pray in the name of God, the Great Mother. Amen.

February 21

Hagar the Egyptian, the Only Person in the Bible to Call God by Name, Genesis 16:1–15; 21:1–21; 25:12

HOLY GOD OF SEEING, we come before you admitting our condemnation of the political system that allowed this woman to be enslaved, impregnated, and then cast out with her child at her mistress's will. We recall the patriarch's passivity throughout Sarah's mistreatment of Hagar. We praise you for the courage and perception Hagar showed when she called you by name in the desert. We thank you for promising Hagar that her line would become a great nation. We ask you to comfort those who are oppressed by circumstances or relationships, especially women with children. Help us stand with them and lighten their burdens during their distress. For we pray in the name of the Lord, whose ancestors you led out of bondage in Egypt. Amen.

February 24

Anne B., Co-Founder of Al-Anon Family Group, 1984

HOLY TRINITY, we praise you for our sister Anne, and for her concern for the families of alcoholics. For many years she, Lois W., and other wives of alcoholics supported one another through the ups and downs of living with husbands in various stages of recovery from alcoholism. We give you thanks that her friendship with Lois led finally to the founding of Al-Anon Family Group. Many families have found support because of Anne and Lois's willingness to share the support group they developed through the years. We ask for your continued strength for all of us who are in any way affected by alcohol or substance abuse. For we pray in the name of Jesus, the Vine. Amen.

February 28

Martyrs in the Plague of Alexandria, **Died Nursing the Sick and Dying, 261**

HOLY PHYSICIAN OF LIFE, we praise you for the compassion and courage of the third-century Christians of Alexandria who risked and lost their own lives by nursing the sick and dying during the plague of Alexandria. We lift up all medical staff and family caregivers who tend those with contagious diseases, especially the incurable ones, as well as all those infected with—or affected by—these illnesses. During times of greatest risk, remind them of the martyrs of Alexandria. Help the medics and caregivers balance reasonable precaution with maintaining a caring relationship, particularly when they are tired or rushed or emotionally distraught. For we pray in the name of the Lord who died and rose to new life. Amen.

March 1

Queen of Sheba, **1 Kings 10**

HOLY ONE, we praise you for the Queen of Sheba, who has been claimed by people of Yemen and Ethiopia. She demonstrated her business acumen, strength, and wisdom by making the long journey from her country to Jerusalem to work out a trade agreement for her people. Although she was curious, she also wanted to test this king, who was known for his wisdom and wealth. We respect her asking hard questions and wanting to prove whether what she had heard about King Solomon was true. Whatever her personal relationship with Solomon, she is a model of a ruler who understood the benefit of wisdom, international trade, and cultural exchange. Amen.

March 2

Ding Ling, **Writer and "Mother" to the New China, 1986**

MOTHER SPIRIT, we praise you for Ding Ling's struggle for women's rights and for the poor. We also thank you for the creativity and courage she showed in her revolutionary writings of protest. Despite the murders of her husband and many friends, she persisted in writing honestly about the conditions of women and the poor during the various political upheavals. Ding Ling had the courage to continue writing even when she was sent to a work farm and her writings were banned. We praise you that even the brutality of the Cultural Revolution was unable to break Ding Ling's spirit. May her inner strength and determination be a model for us. Amen.

March 10

Harriet Tubman, Abolitionist, The Moses of her People, 1913

JESUS, we praise you for your amazing daughter, Harriet, who is rightfully called "The Moses of her People" for her work in the Underground Railroad. Although she suffered brutality that left her physically disabled, she still dared to escape. We praise you for Harriet's courageous efforts to free her people from slavery. We recall that she saved 756 slaves on one momentous occasion and, during the American Civil War, she managed her military intelligence missions so effectively that she gained the respect of generals. Harriet is so much larger than life, it's hard to imagine asking for the kind of inner strength she had. Yet violence still abounds in our world, and so we ask for the ingenuity and daring to risk our very selves as Harriet did to save our sisters and brothers from brutality. For we pray in the name of Jesus, who was beaten and humiliated, and yet died and rose to new life. Amen.

March 19

St. Joseph of Nazareth, Jesus' Father Figure

MOTHERLY FATHER, we praise you for Joseph's loving fatherly care of Jesus, regardless of whether he was Jesus' biological father or not. We thank you for his willingness to marry Mary, despite her pregnancy, and to take responsibility for Jesus. We extol Joseph's openness to your guidance and his protectiveness towards Mary and Jesus. We mourn his early death and wish we knew more about the life of this extraordinary man, yet we celebrate the creative gifts he would have used in his trade, and the model of fatherhood he provided for Jesus. Whether we are male or female, help us to be compassionate to those in distress and to reflect Joseph's trust in you when times are rough. We especially lift up parent-child relationships where there is no shared blood. Help such families build loving relationships by choice. For we pray in the name of Jesus, who through the power of the Holy Spirit became the son of Mary and Joseph. Amen.

March 20 (21)

International Day of Women and the Vernal Equinox

GREAT MOTHER AND FATHER OF ALL, we praise you for the people who saw the need for an International Day of Women and had the influence to establish it. Just as all of nature awakens in the spring and turns the bleakness of winter into an artist's dream, help all women to flourish wherever they are. We especially lift up those who are paying the price for challenging harsh political or religious conditions. Comfort and empower them to do what they must. We join with our sisters throughout the world in praying that together we can turn oppressive, demoralizing situations into joyful, life-giving ones. Guide and bless our efforts to support them. For it is in the name of the Messiah who was born of a woman we pray. Amen.

March 24

Archbishop Oscar Romero, **Martyr of San Salvador, 1980**

MERCIFUL AND JUST GOD, we praise you for empowering your son Oscar to be a "voice for the voiceless" of El Salvador. We note that he spent most of his life as a quietly faithful priest with no sign of the prophet he was to become. While lamenting the assassination of the Jesuit, Rutilio Grande, because of his commitment to social justice, Oscar channeled his grief over Rutilio's murder into action by continuing Rutilio's work for justice. We proclaim Oscar's clear vision of the church's role in standing with the poor and condemning injustice. Give us the love and courage to stand beside those in our communities and in the world who are in need. Help us to discern whether our call is to be a voice for the voiceless or an advocate for the powerless, so they may speak for themselves and be heard. Enable us to stand with our sisters and brothers despite the cost. Amen.

March 25

Mary Joyfully Accepts Becoming Jesus' Mother (The Annunciation), **Luke 1:46–55**

HOLY GOD, we praise you for our sister, Mary, and for her joyful acceptance of your request to become Jesus' mother. We celebrate her response that has been handed down to us in the words of the Magnificat. We acknowledge Mary's willingness to become pregnant before she was married despite the threat to her life. We remember all women who are pregnant, both those who are thrilled and those who are not. We ask, in the name of Mary's son, that you be with them and guide them in the choices they have to make. Amen.

March 26 (24)

Wanda Lee, **Spiritual Gifts of Divination and Encouragement in her Craft Community, 1993**

HOLY MYSTERY, we praise you for Wanda and for her support of her Craft Community. Her spiritual gifts of divination and encouragement were an inspiration to many. Thank you for the generous way she shared her gifts to bring others into harmony with you and your creation. Help us trust ourselves and share the gifts you have given us for the benefit of all. For we pray in the name of the Creator and Lover of All. Amen.

March 28 (30)

Abigail Powers Fillmore, **Teacher, First Lady of U.S.A., 1850–1853, wife of Millard Fillmore, 13th President, 1853**

HOLY GOD, we praise you for your daughter, Abigail, and for her determination and strength of will. Defying the conventions of her time, she married the man of her choice before he could provide for her, and continued teaching after her marriage. Yet this little-known couple became the First Lady and President of the United States. When we make choices that go against expectations, help us to remember Abigail's example. For we pray in the name of a Savior who followed the spirit of the law, rather than its letter. Amen.

April 2

The Syro-Phoenician or Canaanite Woman, **Matthew 9:20–21; Mark 7:25; Luke 8:43–48**

MOTHER SPIRIT, we praise you for your nameless Syro-Phoenician daughter. A fiercely devoted and loving mother, she prevailed upon Jesus—a Jewish teacher and a stranger to her—to cast a demon out of her daughter. Thank you for the woman's persistence in doing what was necessary for her daughter's well-being. We especially praise you that she did not give up when Jesus refused her at first, but continued to reason with him until he changed his mind and did what she asked of him. When we feel like outsiders and hit obstacles as we try to help others, remind us of the Syro-Phoenician Woman. Give us the words to touch the hearts of those with the power to make changes to benefit those in need. Amen.

April 5

Pandita Ramabai, **"Mother of Modern India," Indian Christian Advocate of Women and the Poor, Valued Indian Culture, 1922**

GOD OF LOVE, we praise you for your servant Pandita and for her great love of her fellow women and their children. We thank you for her parents, for what she learned from them, and for how those experiences influenced her life's work. We applaud her efforts in trying to change the custom of marrying young girls off to older men and in caring for the numerous widows and orphans that resulted from such arrangements. We celebrate her independence of spirit and her willingness to struggle with how to be a Christian and an Indian, despite criticism from both sides. Strengthen us when we are faced with difficult choices and remind us of Pandita's persistence in putting her faith into loving action. Amen.

April 9

Sacajawea, **Guide with the Lewis and Clark Expedition, 1884**

GREAT SPIRIT, we praise you for the fearless hospitality with which this Shoshonean woman and her village befriended the two American explorers. Sacajawea's knowledge of the terrain and territory was invaluable. We thank you that she was strong enough to undertake such a journey when she was pregnant. Her fortitude in giving birth along the way and then carrying on is remarkable. Be with all women travelers, especially those who are pregnant. Surround them with your loving strength and comfort when their babies are born. For we pray in the name of Jesus, whose pregnant mother traveled to Bethlehem and gave birth to him there in a manger. Amen.

April 11

Rabi'a al-'Adawiyaa **of Iraq, Sufi (Islamic) Mystic, 801 (185 after Hijra)**

ALLAH AL-ASMA' AL-HUSNA, GOD OF THE BEAUTIFUL NAMES, we praise you for your servant Rabi'a and for her great love of you. At a time and place when most women married, she had the courage to choose you instead. We also appreciate the legends that describe the light of your *sakina,* or presence, that surrounded her head when she prayed. Rabi'a's love poetry to you, her heavenly bridegroom, encourages us to develop an intimate relationship with you, too. May we love you as she did. For we pray in the name of the God of Love. Amen.

April 14

Rachel Carson, **Mother of the Modern Environmental Movement, 1964**

COSMIC CREATOR OF ALL, we praise you for the scientific abilities that led to Rachel's groundbreaking research into the causes of water pollution. We also applaud her courage in giving up her government job so she was free to write about the necessity of caring for the Earth. Her contributions to the environmental movement and her sense of wonder at the beauty of creation encourage us to continue her work. Inspire us to put our respect for the Earth and, indeed, for the Universe into action. For we pray in the name of the Life-Giver. Amen.

April 16

Mirra Loxvickaja, **Poet, about 1904**

HOLY SPIRIT, we praise you for Mirra's creativity and honesty in writing poetry. We also give thanks that she saw the need for silent women to speak up. We abhor the practice of trivializing a woman's creative talents because of its sensuality. We especially laud Mirra for giving women their own voice, and a vivid, sensuous voice at that. In the name of Jesus, who was himself a living, breathing, sensual being. Amen.

April 17

Blessed Kateri Tekakwitha, **the Lily of the Mohawks, 1680**

HOLY SPIRIT, we praise you for the miracle of young Kateri's survival when her family died of smallpox. We thank you for being with her during her marriage, especially when she chose to become a Christian, though it cost her her family and friends. We also note her courage in trekking 200 miles to reach a Christian village where she could live out her days in holiness and simplicity. We wonder if her harsh fasting and mortification were physical ways of expressing her grief over the deaths of her family and her separation from her village. Strengthen those who have to make difficult choices, especially those who are becoming sick over their situations. When we are tempted to neglect our health for the sake of our faith or societal expectations, send us wise and discerning guides. For we pray in the name of Jesus, who took time to himself when he needed to get away from the crowds. Amen.

April 18

Martha, **A Persian Martyr, about 341**

KING OF KINGS, we praise you for the faith and courageous witness of Martha, one of the Persian martyrs. Although we deplore the political conditions that led to the forcible re-settlement of so many people, we are glad Martha's father, Posi, settled enough to marry the Persian woman who became Martha's mother. We mourn the deaths of Martha, Posi, and others who were persecuted simply because they shared the faith of the Persian Empire's enemy. During times of tumult and war, help us to continue loving our neighbors regardless of their faiths and ethnicities. We pray that we may be as strong as Martha was in the conviction of your love for us, and that, when called, we may witness to your great love whatever the personal cost. Amen.

April 21

Lu Meiniang, **Craftswoman, Parasol Designer and Maker, Tang dynasty, about 791**

COSMIC CREATOR, we praise you for Meiniang's intellectual and creative gifts. She was renown for her skill in intricate embroidery work and designing and making exquisite parasol covers. She decorated each parasol cover with over a thousand figures, including the continent and three islands, a god and a goddess, a unicorn and a phoenix. The parasol covers were known as Flying Immortal Covers because the paste Meiniang used enabled the covers to twist like small dragons and so sturdy they were virtually unbreakable. We are impressed that she chose the simple life of a Taoist ascetic instead of the riches the emperor offered in appreciation of her talents. Meiniang's choice led to her new name Xiaoyao ("free and unfettered"). When we are faced with difficult decisions, strengthen us to choose the way of peaceful living. Amen.

April 23

Margaret Fell Fox, Organizational and Pastoral Care Leader of the Quakers, 1702

DIVINE LIGHT, we praise you for Margaret's role in shaping Quakerism throughout the fifty years she was a Friend. We note Margaret's gifts of hospitality, organization, and compassion, which she developed as a wife and mother of eight. We thank you for Margaret's husband, a judge, who accepted her active involvement in the new movement, regardless of the difficulties it meant for his career. We appreciate your leading George Fox, an inspired itinerant preacher with few other skills, to Margaret, a woman of social standing, who could support and care for the new Quakers who were left leaderless, suffering for their faith. Margaret provided a meeting place and basic necessities to those who were imprisoned. We extol Margaret for having the courage of her convictions, even when it meant she herself would be imprisoned. We pray in the name of the Messiah, who had compassion for the thief on the cross next to him. Amen.

April 28

Amos, Prophet, Advocate for Social Justice, 8th century B.C.E.

GOD OF MERCY AND JUSTICE, we praise you for your prophet Amos and the powerful message you gave the world through him. He spoke your words of justice for the poor even though he was denounced and exiled for it. Thank you for Amos's example of speaking for the poor and his courage in challenging the religious leaders of his day. Empower us, as you did Amos, to stand with those without power or voice in our society. For it's in your holy name, we pray. Amen.

May 3

The Woman with a Flow of Blood, Matthew 9:20–22; Mark 5:25–34; Luke 8:43–48

HOLY JESUS, we remember this woman who is called by her illness instead of her name. We sympathize with her misery in menstruating for twelve years, and we weep for the years of loneliness and isolation that the religious laws of her day required her to endure. We praise you for her courage and faith in touching your garment to be healed. We appreciate your sensitivity to her touch. We are especially glad you publicly proclaimed her faith when you healed her. Heal those who are experiencing health problems or are lonely and isolated, we pray. Help us care for our relationships and ourselves as you cared for this brave woman, for it is in your name we ask. Amen.

May 4

Monica, Mother of Augustine of Hippo, 387

JESUS OUR BROTHER, we praise you for the life and faith of Monica, Augustine's mother. Surely Monica's heart ached because of some of the choices her son made. Just as the Spirit comforted and strengthened your mother during the puzzling times of your life, and especially in her grief at your death, we thank you for sending the Holy Comforter to Monica when she was distressed by her son's behavior. Allay our fears when our children or young friends and relatives struggle with hard choices. Give us the discernment to know when to advise gently, when to keep quiet, and when to speak up. For we pray in the name of a son whose mother experienced both extreme pain and great joy because of the choices they made in response to the Divine Call. Amen.

May 8

Dame Julian of Norwich, Mystic, about 1417

MOTHERLY FATHER, we praise you for the faithfulness of your servant, Julian, and for the richness of the divine revelations you gave her. We are amazed that she spent twenty years contemplating them before recording them. When we recall her long contemplation of those revelations, as well as the five centuries it took for people to become interested in them, we have an idea of what it means to wait on you. Give us the patience to wait on you in the fullness of your time. For it is in the name of Jesus we pray. Amen.

May 16

Dymphna, Patron of Epileptics and the Mentally Ill, about 650

GOD OF WHOLENESS, we praise you that Dymphna had the courage to flee her abusive father, though we're horrified that he actually murdered her when he caught up. We give thanks for the people with epilepsy and mental illnesses who were healed by being near her tomb. We rejoice that the stigma of epilepsy and mental illness is diminishing. We lift up all those who have fled violent relationships and those who have struggled with epilepsy and mental illnesses. Give us the wisdom and strength to work for healthful relationships in our families and in our communities. Amen.

May 22

Martha Dandridge Custis Washington, **First Lady of the U.S.A., 1789–1797, Wife of George Washington, 1st President, 1802**

GRACIOUS GOD, we praise you for your daughter, Martha, and her place in the history of the United States. Since Martha was not temperamentally suited for the public life she was expected to lead as general's wife, her willingness to join her husband and the troops at Valley Forge during the Revolutionary War is remarkable. We also thank you for the children Martha bore during her first marriage. Though we sympathize over her children's early deaths, we are thankful for the grandchildren who supported her in later life. When we find ourselves in uncomfortable situations, help us to remember Martha's efforts to make the best of it. For we pray in the name of God, who can be heard in a still small voice. Amen.

May 24

Bilhah, **Genesis 30:6,** *Zilpah,* **Genesis 30:11, and** *All Surrogate Mothers*

MERCIFUL GOD, we remember Bilhah and Zilpah and their forgotten roles as the biological mothers to four of the tribes of Israel. We reject the practice of polygamy that pitted Rachel and Leah against each other and condemn the patriarchal system that enabled Rachel and Leah to give their respective maids to their husband, Jacob, to produce more sons. Nevertheless we praise you that Bilhah and Zilpah were able to raise their sons, and that their sons were counted among the twelve tribes of Israel. We lift up all kinds of blended families, especially women who become surrogate mothers for economic reasons. We also give thanks for the women in our lives who are like mothers to us, regardless of how the relationship developed. Amen.

May 25

Wang Zhenyi, **Scientist, Qing dynasty, 1797**

SOURCE OF ALL, we praise you for Wang Zhenyi and for her wide-ranging intellectual abilities. Although she made outstanding contributions in the fields of mathematics and astronomy, she also was known for her poems. Help us to value both the arts and sciences, as Wang Zhenyi did, so we as individuals and our society itself may become more balanced. Amen.

May 29

The Visitation of Mary to Elizabeth, Luke 1:35–56

MOTHERLY FATHER, we praise you that the young Mary had a warm, loving older cousin to visit when she needed some guidance during the early stages of her pregnancy. We rejoice with the elderly Elizabeth who became pregnant at last. We give thanks for the bond that developed between them and their babies. We are thankful that you worked through the ordinary ways of women to do something extraordinary in both a young woman and an older one. We lift up women of childbearing ages and ask you to watch over them whether they have no children or many. We ask you to guide and bless them and their families, both immediate and extended. For we pray in the name of the God who is the Mother and Father of us all. Amen.

May 31

Those Who Have Experienced Armed Conflict

LOVING GOD, we remember all those who have experienced armed conflict, whether in the military or as civilians. Most especially we lift up those whose living conditions are so desperate they see fighting as the only way to a better life. We ask for dramatic changes for those who feel so hopeless. We lift up those who have been injured in war, whether physically, emotionally, or spiritually. We also ask for healing for the families of those who were killed, and for the injured and their families. We remember the damage done to the ecosystems during times of war, and ask for healing for Mother Earth and Father Sky. For we pray in the name of the Prince of Peace. Amen.

June 4

Jephthah's Daughter, **Judges 11:34–40, A Woman Christ-figure (Her Death Foreshadowed Christ's Death)**

HEAVENLY FATHER, we praise you for the young woman known only as Jephthah's daughter. Although it seems senseless for her to die because of her father's foolhardy vow, we thank you that she was strong enough to claim time for herself to be with her friends before her death. Like the early Syrian Church, we proclaim Jephthah's Daughter as a Christ-figure. While we appreciate having a biblical woman whose death foreshadowed Christ's own death on the cross, we ask you to keep us from using Jesus' death as a reason to ignore life's tragedies. Temper our desire to understand what is behind the trials of this life with an urge to work for justice now. For we pray in the name of your Son, who died and rose to new life. Amen.

June 9

St. Columba, Abbot of Iona, Unofficial Patron of Abused Women and Girls, 597

And *St. Ephrem the Syrian,* Deacon, Hymn-writer for Women's Choirs, 373

SACRED THREE, you sent your servants, Columba and Ephrem, to minister to your people in very different times and places, and yet they both showed love to women and girls. We praise you for Columba's efforts to reduce male violence against females, despite his discomfort with sexuality, and for Ephrem's overwhelming affirmation of women—their faith, their voices, and their choices, whether for celibacy or motherhood. Bless our efforts to end violence of all kinds, especially the violence of rape and abuse. Broaden our vision so we may support all aspects of women's growth and that of ourselves, in the name of God the Mother, who through Jesus, the Living Breast, sustains the world with the Spirit. Amen.

June 10

Founding of the Society of Alcoholics Anonymous, 1935

HIGHER POWER, we praise you for Dr. Bob and Bill W., and their roles in founding Alcoholics Anonymous. We are thankful for the countless people who have benefited from following the Twelve Steps. May those in need of a twelve-step program find a warm welcome and the help they need to reach and maintain sobriety. For we pray in the hope of Serenity. Amen.

June 17

Susanna Wesley, The Moral and Religious Mother of Methodism, 1742

And *Evelyn Underhill,* Mystic, Married London Homemaker, 1941

GREAT MYSTERY, you have worked through two women, both of whom were married homemakers, to achieve very different purposes. While Evelyn's theological studies and contemplation led her into a mystical relationship with you, Susanna's deep faith and orderly, prayerful home life led her and her sons into a new form of worship. We praise you that you can and do work through us whatever our personal circumstances may be. We lift up those who are contemplatives and mystics, along with those who are practical and methodical in their worship, acknowledging the value in all relationships with you. Lead us deeper into your divine presence. Amen.

June 21

Summer Solstice

HEAVENLY LIGHT, we praise you for this, the longest day of the year. As we move toward the solstice, we have more light day by day. After the solstice, we will have more darkness day by day. Thank you for being with us through light and dark. Thank you, too, for creation and the gift of light, physically through the sun, and spiritually through the Light of the World. Amen.

June 22

Female Slave of Phillipi, **Acts 16:16**

ALL-KNOWING GOD, we praise you for the Female Slave of Phillipi, even though so little is known about her. Although in scripture we meet her only in relation to the men in her midst, you know the real woman she was. We celebrate her release from the spirit that controlled her, and her release from her owners. We lift up those who are in bondage of any kind—physical, emotional, or spiritual. Empower each and every one of us to do what's needed to free ourselves and our sisters and brothers who are manipulated by circumstances beyond their control. For we pray in the name of the God of Goodness and Wholeness. Amen.

June 23

Betty Shabazz, **Model of Perseverance, College Official, Civil Rights Leader, 1997**

MERCIFUL GOD, we praise you for Betty and her perseverance. A private person, she played the public role she needed to as the wife and, later, the widow of Malcolm X. She worked hard to raise their six daughters well, to become a registered nurse, and then to earn three university degrees. She reached out to her community, speaking on health education, civil rights, and women's rights, and educating others about the work of Malcolm X. She continued to persevere until the end of her life. When we face hard times, help us to remember Betty's ability to decide what is important and to persevere. For we pray in the name of the Spirit who strengthens us. Amen.

June 25

Sadhu Sundar Singh, **Teacher, Evangelist, and Indian Mystic, 1929**

DIVINE MYSTERY, we praise you for this holy man's gift of seeing Jesus as the link between the wisdom traditions of East and West. We recall his courage in living as a Christian *sadhu,* an itinerant preacher with no possessions. Sundar's emphasis on spending time with you daily is encouraging.

Above all, we thank you that he remained true to his call, despite the criticism and hostility he received. Help us to value the good in different religions, while growing ever closer to you. For we pray in the name of Jesus, the bridge between East and West. Amen.

June 27

***Helen Keller,* Author, Blind, Deaf, Advocate for the Blind and Handicapped, 1880**

GOD OF INNER PEACE, we praise you for this amazing woman's many gifts. We give thanks for her teacher and mentor, Anne Sullivan, who enabled Helen to express herself first by signing and, later, through writing. We admire Helen for reaching out of the silence of deafness and the gloom of blindness to become a strong advocate for blind or handicapped people. Give us the determination to face our limitations head-on, and when possible to overcome them. Regardless of our abilities and gifts, help us share ourselves with others so our community will move towards wholeness. For we pray in the name of the Great Creator. Amen.

July 3

***Enmegahbowh* "One-who-stands-before-his-people," (Ojibwa-Ottawa), Methodist Preacher, First Native American Episcopal Priest, 1902**

HEAVENLY FATHER, we praise you for your faithful witness, Enmegahbowh. We marvel that even before he became a Christian, he was called "One-who-stands-before-his-people." While we deplore the political conditions that used acceptance of the Christian faith as a means of subduing Native Americans and divesting them of their heritage, we celebrate this man's faithfulness and his love for you and his people, first as a Methodist and later as an Episcopal preacher. We also appreciate his bishops' willingness to step out in faith by ordaining a Native American to be a deacon in 1859, and, finally, eight years later in 1867, to ordain him a priest. We ask you to be with those who are called to wait on you. Give them patience when it is necessary, and discernment when action is needed. For we pray in the name of Jesus who waited until he was thirty to leave his work as a carpenter to begin his ministry reconciling people to you. Amen.

July 7

***Fethullah Gulen,* Teacher, Humanitarian, Muslim Cleric, born 1938**

GREAT GOD OF COMPASSION, we praise you for the life and teachings of Fethullah Gulen. We especially appreciate his gifts of starting schools for men and women where both science and Islam are taught in a balanced way. His example of reconciling science and religion is an inspiration. We admire his belief that becoming truly human necessitates learning, teaching, and inspiring others. Inspire us, Merciful One, so we, too, may continue to grow in knowledge and faith. Amen.

July 19

***First Convention for Women's Rights, Declaration of Rights and Sentiments Adopted,* Seneca Falls, NY, 1848, and *Beginning of the Women's Rights Movement in U.S.A.,* 1848**

HOLY MOTHER, we praise you for the tea at which Elizabeth Stanton inspired women to work for women's rights. This simple gathering led to another tea where, instead of tea cakes, issues affecting women's rights were put on the table. These women formulated the Declaration of Sentiments that would be added to and adopted at the First Convention for Women's Rights in Seneca Falls, New York. We praise you for the decades of hard work and the many disappointments these and numerous other women and men experienced in the fight to achieve voting rights for women. Though in years to come, some chose to focus on votes for white women at the expense of women of color, we honor the sacrifices our foremothers made to secure the voting rights that all American women enjoy today. Amen.

July 21

***Sun Bu-Er,* Mother of Three, Taoist Sage, about 1124**

GOD OF WISDOM AND LIGHT, we praise you for the life and example of Sun Bu-Er. At a time when women were restricted to certain roles, she had children as expected, but went on to become a Taoist sage. Help us understand that as we follow the conventional path, we are developing gifts that may be needed later, in new and unexpected ways. For we pray in the name of the God of Surprises. Amen.

July 22

***St. Mary Magdalene,* Apostle and Preacher, Matthew 27:56, 61; 28:1; Mark 15:41, 47; 16:1, 9 Luke 8:2; 24:10; John 19:25; 20:1, 11, 16, 18**

HOLY REDEEMER, we praise you for your disciple, St. Mary Magdalene, and the close relationship she had with you. We celebrate the tradition in art and oral history that credited Mary Magdalene with consecrating Lazarus as the bishop of Marseilles, and recognized her apostolic authority when she preached to the frightened male apostles. Help both women and men to witness to your goodness and authority in creation, even when it means radical ways of thinking. For it is in your name we pray. Amen.

July 27

St. Mechtild of Magdeburg, **Mystic, Prophet, about 1282**

GREAT MYSTERY, we praise you for your servant Mechtild and for the intimate relationship she had with you throughout her long life. We remember her persistence and bravery in speaking out against corrupt priests, the most powerful men of her day, despite the harm that came to her as a result. Help us to be as prayerful and as persistent and brave when we are faced with similar calls to action, in the name of the Lord who challenged the religious authorities of his day. Amen.

July 28

Martha of Bethany, Evangelist, and Her Sister, Mary, **John 11:17–44**

PRECIOUS BROTHER, in your great compassion for Martha's and Mary's grief over the death of their brother, you show us that a man's tears are as natural as a woman's, and that the anger that comes with grief can become the rock of faith. Help us break down the barriers to wholeness that have caused women to be either frenzied doers or passive listeners. Readjust our sense of balance so each of us may value who we really are. Confirm our belief in you so that, even in times of sore distress, we may proclaim with Martha, "You are the Christ." For we ask in your name, Jesus, with the Mother-Father and the Holy Spirit. Amen.

August 1

Lady Song, **Three Kingdoms period, Scholar, 364**

FOUNTAIN OF LIFE, we praise you for Lady Song and her intellectual gifts. She lived at a time when scholars' families were expected to memorize entire volumes to preserve them in case the writings were burned or banned during political turmoil. For memorizing the classic *The Rituals of Zhou* on the Zhou government's reconstruction system, she was called Perpetuator of Civilization. At the age of eighty Lady Song was given the job of teaching the Zhou rituals and their interpretations to 120 students. She was admired for her inner integrity, loyalty, love of her country, and altruism. Like Lady Song, help us honor our heritages despite the unrest of modern life. Amen.

August 2

Um Kolthom, **Egyptian Singer, 1975**

COMPASSIONATE GOD, we praise you for Um Kolthom's awe-inspiring voice and for giving her the opportunity to share her musical gifts. Her singing touched many hearts throughout the world. Like Um Kolthom, help us to use whatever gifts you have given us to benefit others. For we pray in your holy name. Amen.

August 6

The Transfiguration of the Beloved Son, **Matthew 17:1–8; Mark 9:2–8; Luke 9:28–36**

SACRED THREE, we praise you for sharing the transfiguration of Jesus with those three disciples and so with us. We thank you for the messages of personal comfort Jesus may have received from Moses and Elijah's appearance, assuring him of your presence and power in the difficult times ahead. We realize that for Jesus, a fully human male, fear and uncertainty would be a natural experience, so we appreciate your tender care in being present with him during his time of distress. We also praise you for sending Elijah as a preview of what was to come in Jesus' resurrection. We hope that Jesus was able to draw strength from the man, who with your help, resurrected the son of the widow of Zarephath. Since you gave new life to her son, surely you would do the same for Mary's child, and your only begotten son. In the Transfiguration Jesus' place in the law and the prophetic tradition of his people is made manifest. We praise you for letting us see the big picture as well as part of the smaller, more intimate one. Amen.

August 11

St. Clare, Abbess at Assisi, **Founder of the Poor Clares, 1253**

And *St. Mary, The Mother of Jesus,* **1st century, Luke 1:26–56; 2:1–7, 16–19**

HOLY GOD, we praise you for Clare and Mary, one single, one a mother. When faced with your call, both said yes to you, the God of love. Whether we are called, like Clare, to be single and childless, or like Mary, to be mothers, help us live our lives lovingly and faithfully. Empower us to respond yes to your call so your love may abound in this world and the next, in the name of Jesus, Mary's son, and the power of the Holy Spirit who overshadowed Mary and empowered Clare. Amen.

August 20

Bernard of Clairvaux, **Abbot, Poet, Hebraist in France, 1153**

LORD JESUS, we praise you for this man and his love for you and respect for your heritage. At a time when his contemporaries were condemning the local Jewish community, Bernard was open enough to see the spirit of holiness in Hebrew literature. We praise you for his example of tolerance of others and appreciation for their holy writings. Help us to see you in all people, and to treat followers of other religions, and those who do not follow a religion, with respect. For it is in your name we pray. Amen.

August 31

Aidan, **Bishop of Lindisfarne, England, Patron of Arts, Mentor to Abbesses, 651**

BLESSED TRINITY, we praise you for Aidan's gentle compassion and for his example of servant leadership. We extol Aidan's encouragement of the arts that led to the creation of the Lindisfarne Gospels. We especially celebrate his willingness to mentor strong women of faith like the Abbesses Bega of St. Bees, Hilda of Whitby, Ebba of St. Abbs, and Ethelreda of Ely. Guide the leaders of our faith communities to follow Aidan's example so that men and women may use their diverse gifts to glorify you. For we pray in the name of the Creator of the universe. Amen.

September 1

David Pendleton Oakerhater (a.k.a. Oakenhater, "O-kuh-ha-tuh") "Making Medicine" **(Cheyenne), 1931**

GREAT SPIRIT, we praise you for the faithfulness of your servant, David Pendleton Oakerhater. We recall that although prejudice denied him ordination to the priesthood, he continued to serve you among his people as a deacon for 50 years. We abhor the fear and apathy toward Native Americans that led the Episcopal Church to overlook David's saintly example for over 50 years, yet we celebrate his far-reaching ministry on the reservation. We lift up all those who are working under harsh conditions and ask you to bless them. Give us the sensitivity to look beyond ourselves to see your face in unexpected places and peoples. For we pray in the name of the One who was born in a manger. Amen.

September 5

***The Pankhurst Family:* Mother, *Emmeline,* 1928, and Father, *Richard,* 1898, and their Daughters, *Christabel,* 1958, *Sylvia,* 1960, and *Adela,* 1961, Militant Women's Rights Advocates**

GOD OF MERCY AND JUSTICE, we praise you for Emmeline and Richard and their three daughters, Christabel, Sylvia, and Adela, who worked so valiantly for equal rights for women. We recall the legal and social oppression that British women experienced and extol the Pankhursts for wanting to change the system. We also appreciate Richard for drafting some of the first bills for women's rights, and we admire Emmeline for including their daughters in the fight. We thank you for this family's perseverance and continued efforts despite the slow progress, and for their courage in facing harsh sentences for the sake of their political beliefs. For it's in the name of Jesus we pray. Amen.

September 6

***Bega,* Founder of St. Bee's Monastery, Gave to the Poor and Oppressed, 7th century**

SACRED THREE, we praise you for your daughter Bega. Her courage in crossing the Irish Channel to Cumbria was matched by her compassion in helping the poor and oppressed people on both sides of the Scottish-English border. We proclaim Bega's strong leadership of her own community and rejoice that she was respected enough to substitute for St. Hilda of Whitby when her duties as abbess took her away from the convent. We marvel that in the 7th century, when travel was difficult, Bega assembled a circle of brilliant abbesses, all disciples of Aidan of Lindisfarne, to support one another. When we are tempted to take on excessive responsibility or to go it alone, remind us of Bega and the others in her circle of abbesses (Hilda of Whitby, Ebba of St. Abbs, and Ethelreda of Ely). Encourage us to support one another in our callings as they did. Give us teachers like Aidan to nurture our continued spiritual growth. For we pray in the name of Jesus, who sent the Holy Spirit to empower and comfort us. Amen.

September 9

***Sidqi* of Turkey, Sufi Poet, Mystic, Celibate, 1703**

HOLY MYSTERY, we praise you for your daughter, Sidqi. Her love of you is still thrilling, even three centuries after she lived. We thank you that her love poetry to you has been preserved and translated, blessing countless people with its beauty. Sidqi's spiritual love affair with you excites us to enter into a fuller relationship with the Divine. We pray in the name of our Compassionate, Merciful Lover. Amen.

September 10

Blessed Teresa **of Calcutta, Founder of the Missionaries of Charity, 1997**

LOVING GOD, we praise you for your daughter, Teresa, and for her great love of your people. We are amazed that such a petite woman had the strength to do such great things. Although critics have censured her for not trying to change the political system that allows such poverty, we thank you that she was so secure in her calling to love the "unlovable" that their words did not deflect her. Like Mother Teresa, help us to see you wherever we are. Strengthen our devotion to you so that we are not distracted by naysayers. Grant to those with the power to improve the lives of so many the inspiration to use that power effectively. For we pray in the name of Jesus, who commands us to feed his flock. Amen.

September 11

9/11/01

Shanksville, Pa., United Airlines #93; South Tower WTC, United Airlines #175; North Tower WTC, American Airlines #11; Pentagon, American Airlines #77

GOD OF MERCY AND JUSTICE, in the beginning, you created all of creation and saw that it was good. Then on this day in 2001, you felt the destruction and wounding of thousands of your children when the four hijacked planes were brutally used as weapons. We cherish the memories of those who died and lift up those who were wounded, physically, emotionally, or spiritually. You know the whys and wherefores that have led to the distortion of a religion of peace.

In another time of suffering, you said through your servant Jeremiah (31:13), "I will turn their mourning into joy, I will comfort them, and give them gladness for sorrow." We lift up everyone who was and still is affected by the choices the hijackers and their supporters made on this day in 2001. May your will be done, on earth as it is in heaven. For we pray through the power of the Holy Spirit in the name of God the Mother-Father, whose only-begotten Son was crucified yet rose to new life. Amen.

September 15

Feng Liao, **Diplomat and Ambassador for Han dynasty, 50 B.C.E.**

SOURCE OF ALL, we praise you for Feng Liao and her diplomatic skills. We thank you that she was able to serve Han China as an ambassador for so long. During her fifty years as ambassador to Wusun, she encouraged unity and friendship between her people and the minorities who lived south of the Tianshan Mountains. Her example inspires us to seek unity and to be friends to the foreigners in our midst. Amen.

September 18

Dag Hammarskjold, **Secretary General of the U.N., 1961**

LOVING GOD, we praise you for your servant Dag and for his fervent commitment to peace. We admire his courage in undertaking negotiations despite the danger involved, and thank you that he lived to finish his journal, which has inspired numerous people around the world. Strengthen us to work for peace in our world. For we pray in the name of the Giver of Absolute Peace. Amen.

September 23

Autumnal Equinox

CREATOR OF THE UNIVERSE, we praise you for this day, which marks the midpoint between the shortest and the longest days of the year. We celebrate the workings of the Earth and its place in the solar system. We recall the traditions of harvest festivals to thank you for providing food for the winter. Help us depend on you for our sustenance and enable us to live in harmony with the earth and all creation. For we pray in the name of the Life-Giver. Amen.

September 29

St. Michael and All Angels, **Daniel 10**

FATHERLY MOTHER, on the very first day Daniel cried out for help, you responded by sending Michael and another angel to him. When we are afraid and impatient, remind us that it took the angels twenty-one days to get to Daniel because they were fighting spiritual forces that were beyond his knowledge or experience. Michael's persistence in coming to Daniel's aid reminds us that you have heard our pleas and responded immediately. We ask for patience as we wait for your angels to reach us. Help us recognize the angels you send and to respond to their messages from you. We thank you for their perceptiveness and willingness to say over and over throughout the ages, "Do not be afraid. God sent me to you." Open our eyes so that, like your angels, we may see the fear in our neighbors' hearts and alleviate it with your love, through the power of the Holy Spirit. Amen.

October 1

National Breast Cancer Awareness Month

LIVING BREAST, we praise you for the people who established the month of October as National Breast Cancer Awareness Month. We also thank you for the many lives that have been saved or extended because women and men are becoming aware that early detection matters. Inspire us to take care of ourselves, physically, mentally, and spiritually. Amen.

October 3

Agneta Chang, **A Maryknoll Sister, Founder of the Sisters of Our Lady of Perpetual Help in North Korea, Martyr, 1950**

GREAT LOVER OF LIFE, we praise you for the life and witness of Agneta Chang, a Maryknoll sister. We recall her faithfulness and courage in founding the Sisters of Our Lady of Perpetual Help in North Korea during World War II, despite the isolation and danger. We thank you for being with this woman from the South who became the leader of a newly formed community in the North after her country was divided. We thank you for being with her during the many traumas the division of her country caused, especially during her last days, when religious communities were banned by the Communists and Agneta was shot and burned along with other women. Strengthen the faith of all who live in dangerous places, and guide us in supporting them in their struggle for justice and freedom. For we pray in the name of our Lord, who suffered the brutality of crucifixion before he was raised to new life. Amen.

October 4

St. Francis of Assisi, **Friar, Founder of the Franciscans, 1226**

GREAT CREATOR, we praise you for your servant, Francis, and for his great love of your creation. We thank you for his choosing a life of service and simplicity over the life of selfishness that his family's wealth enabled. We thank you, too, that he accepted Clare's call to live a single life devoted to you, while encouraging married couples to serve you faithfully in a different way. Francis' ability to see you in all of creation reminds us to cherish Mother Earth. He showed his appreciation of a woman's spiritual gifts by appointing Clare to lead the female branch of the Franciscans. From Francis's and Clare's examples we see that women and men can value one another and live in harmony. Help us to follow their examples in loving you, your creation, and one another faithfully, in the name of the Holy Spirit, who inspires us to love. Amen.

October 5

Lois W., **Co-Founder of Al-Anon Family Group, 1988**

HOLY TRINITY, we praise you for our sister, Lois, and her concern for the families of alcoholics. For many years she, Anne B., and other wives of alcoholics supported each other through the ups and downs of living with husbands in various stages of recovery from alcoholism. We give you thanks that her friendship with Anne B. led to the founding of Al-Anon Family Group. Many families have found strength and courage because of Lois and Anne's willingness to share the support group with others. We ask for your continued strength for all of us who are in any way affected by alcohol or substance abuse. For we pray in the name of Jesus, the Bread of Life. Amen.

October 7

Rubye Doris Smith Robinson, **Leader of the Student Non-Violent Coordinating Committee, 1967**

GOD OF MERCY AND JUSTICE, we praise you for your daughter, Rubye, and for her gifts of organization and determination. We are thankful for all she accomplished in her twenty-four years, before her life was cut short by cancer. Though she and the S.N.C.C. preferred non-violence, they knew first-hand how hard it is to live that way. We thank you for Rubye's self-respect and for her ability to encourage others to stand tall, even in the face of prejudice. When we come across injustice, help us remember this brilliant young woman so we, too, may work to right the wrongs of society. For we pray in the name of the Spirit who strengthens us. Amen.

October 9

Anna Freud, **Pioneer Child Psychologist, 1982**

And ***National Depression Screening Day***

LOVING GOD, we praise you for the pioneering work of Anna in advancing our understanding of child development and for those who established a nation-wide screening day for people who may suffer from depression. Just as Anna's research and loving care helped many children become healthier, so this National Depression Screening Day has enabled many people to get the mental health care they need. When we, or our children, are dealing with depression or other mental health problems, give us the clarity of mind or strength of spirit to get help. Amen.

October 16

Sarah Winnemucca Hopkins, **Interpreter, Teacher, Advocate for Native American Rights, 1891**

GREAT SPIRIT, we praise you for Sarah's communication skills and teaching abilities. We also thank you for her commitment to improving the lives of her people through her work for Native American rights. Her efforts inspired others who came after her. Enable us to hear the message she gave and to act on it, so Native Americans may live in dignity and harmony. Amen.

October 18

St. Luke the Evangelist **Luke 1–2**

HEAVENLY HEALER, you worked through Luke, the physician, to teach us about our Lord's childhood and to show us what it means to be a family. We, as women, give you our most heartfelt thanks for choosing a man who valued women and children to spread the Good News. We—and our families—are strengthened because Luke cared enough about Jesus' infancy to record it. We lift up all those who care for the health of families, and ask you to bless those who follow Luke's example and to enlighten those who do not, in the name of Jesus, the Great Medicine of Life, in the power of the Mother Spirit. Amen.

October 24 (23)

St. James the Just of Jerusalem, **Jesus' Brother, Martyr, about 62, Galatians 1:19**

MOTHERLY FATHER, we praise you for James, who was known as James the Just, James of Jerusalem, and also as James, the brother of our Lord Jesus. We thank you that James was a just man and that he became a leader of the early church in his own right. We recall the emphasis he put on prayer and his efforts to reconcile those who were in conflict. We lament the attitude of those in the church who thought it better to remember James as Jesus' cousin rather than as his brother, so their Mother Mary could be proclaimed ever virgin, her sexuality denied. We wonder how it felt for James to be Jesus' brother, much less the brother of the crucified and resurrected anointed one of God. Growing up in a family with an older brother or sister is not always easy, so we thank you that Jesus and James were able to put aside childhood rivalries and develop their own faith and talents. We are thankful, too, that James was active enough in the early church to be known as Jesus' brother because he and their younger brothers and sisters confirm Mary and Jesus' full humanity. We pray in the name of the Holy Trinity, the ultimate model for family life. Amen.

October 26

Women's Rights Advocates *Elizabeth Cady Stanton,* Biblical Scholar, Writer, 1902

And *Susan B. Anthony,* Orator, 1906

DIVINE FEMININE, we praise you for these amazing women and their tremendous efforts to persuade enough men to amend the constitution to allow women to vote. We lament their deaths before they themselves could vote. We extol Elizabeth's brilliant scholarship on the way men have misused religion to deny women their place in society and Christianity. We applaud Susan's courageous determination in spreading Elizabeth's message of rights for women. We celebrate the way Susan's oratorical gifts complemented Elizabeth's intellectual insights. Give us the stamina to use our gifts to benefit the voiceless of our society and our religious institutions, especially when, like Elizabeth and Susan, we may not see the end results. For we pray in the Spirit of Wholeness. Amen.

October 27 (28)

***In Commemoration of Anna the Prophet and Evangelist and Simeon the Priest,* Luke 2:36–38**

MOTHERLY FATHER, you fulfilled Anna's and Simeon's desire to see the Messiah before their deaths. Help us wait when we need to wait and to see your glory in our journey in faith when the time for waiting is complete. We praise you for Anna's enthusiasm in preaching the Good News to everyone she met. We also thank you for giving Jesus and Mary the gifts of prophecy and priesthood through Simeon. Remind us that you know our heart's desire. You have precious gifts for us, no matter our age or gender. Give us Anna's exuberance as we share your love with those around us. And like Simeon, let us cherish your amazing gifts and the joy of passing them on to others. For it is in the name of our Lord Jesus we pray, through the power of the Holy Spirit. Amen.

November 2

Commemoration of the Day of the Dead

GREAT SPIRIT, you breathed the soul and very life into the first humans and created them male and female in your own image. We lift up all those who have died, whether their deaths were a natural end to a long life or an abrupt and violent one, as Jesus' was. Hold all grieving families and friends, we pray, in the comforting love of your bosom. We marvel at your life-giving love that conquered death here on earth and forevermore. Help us live in that love. Amen.

November 4

***Raissa Maritain,* Poet and Contemplative, 1960**

ALL-KNOWING OCEAN OF LIFE, we praise you for Raissa's creativity and intimacy with you. We admire her Russian parents' determination to give their exceptional daughters a better education in France, where Raissa later found a soul mate in her husband, Jacques. We marvel at Raissa's resolve to live a contemplative life while engaged in the world, as she realized that we are called "to live in the whirlwind . . . to let ourselves pitch and toss in the waves of the divine will." When we are tempted to jump ship so we can stand on firm ground, give us the security of your presence as a lifesaver around us. Enable us to balance living in the world with moving ever closer to you. For we pray in your holy name. Amen.

November 8

Maria Petrovykh* (1979), Mother, Poet, Editor, Translator, and her daughter, *Arisha Golovacheva

GREAT MOTHER, we praise you for bringing tenderness out of the brutality of Stalin's reign of mass terror. We applaud Maria's belief that she had but one calling, to become Arisha's mother. We extol the fulfilling mother-daughter relationship that inspired Maria to write her two lyric poems to Arisha. We are in awe of Maria's courage in writing poetry with spiritual revelations during such dangerous times. Enable those of us with children to value our calling as mothers, while balancing the other demands on our time. We lift up the people world-wide, especially mothers and their children, who live in fear. Draw near to them and bless their love relationships. For we pray in the name of Jesus, who experienced the brutality of his age, yet continued to love. Amen.

November 16

***Dr. Bob,* Co-Founder of Alcoholics Anonymous, 1950**

HIGHER POWER, we praise you for Dr. Bob's willingness to work with Bill W. in reaching sobriety for himself and for countless others. We also thank you that he was able to use his medical expertise and participation in Alcoholics Anonymous to lead to a better understanding of alcoholism, as he provided caring treatment of alcoholics years before alcoholism was accepted as a disease. We also appreciate Dr. Bob's respect for Sister Ignatia and their ability to work together for the good of their patients. When we are in uncharted territory, guide us to work to your glory and the benefit of others, for we pray in the name of the Empowering Holy Spirit. Amen.

November 17

Audre Lorde, **Black, Lesbian, Mother, Warrior Poet, 1992**

MOTHERLY FATHER, we praise you for the many gifts of Audre, the mother of the spirituality of eroticism and a long-time cancer survivor. Most especially we thank you for her example of accepting herself as she was, for her honesty encourages others to be themselves. Give us the courage to follow Audre's example in accepting all aspects of ourselves, especially our sexuality and our spirituality. For we pray in the name of the One who created male and female and saw that they were good. Amen.

November 18

St. Hilda, **Abbess of Whitby, 680**

GLORIOUS TRINITY, we praise you for your daughter, Hilda, abbess, mother to all who knew her and convenor of the Synod of Whitby. We note her wide-ranging work as an administrator, educator, and spiritual guide. We remember that five of her monks became bishops (Bosta of York, Aetta of Colchester, Ottfor of Worcester, Wilfred II of York, and John of Beverley). We applaud her missionary role in inspiring the first paraphrases of the Bible into the local Anglo-Saxon dialect, giving her a place of honor as a mother of English letters. We affirm her decisive position in the Synod of Whitby, though it helped strengthen the Roman practice at the expense of Celtic forms of Christianity. This remarkable seventh-century woman exercised both political and spiritual authority over large territories, advised governing bodies, and called up soldiers during times of war. Yet she died encouraging her flock to maintain harmony within the Church. Help us, we pray, during times of conflict in our churches and communities, to be good stewards of the talents and authority you've given us as women made in your image. Give us the spirit to discern how to bring about genuine unity while affirming our diversity. Amen.

November 19

Lois Clark **(Creek), Teacher, Author, Instrumental in Establishing Saint's Day for David Oakerhater (a.k.a. Oakenhater), 1985**

JESUS, you broke the conventions of your day to affirm faith when you saw it. We praise you for the life of Lois Clark, a teacher and author, who followed your example and persistently exhorted the National Episcopal Church of the U.S.A. to establish a feast day for David Pendleton Oakerhater. Thank you for giving this petite woman such a dynamic spirit and so strong a sense of the need to proclaim David Oakerhater's witness in our churches. We here and now also proclaim Lois's witness to you and to the Episcopal Church. Help us to speak the truth lovingly, yet firmly, when we are called to do so. We pray in your name, Jesus. Amen.

November 20 (16)

St. Margaret, Queen of Scotland, Mother, Advocate for Social Justice, 1093

HOLY ONE, we praise you for your daughter Margaret, a queen who served the people of Scotland. We thank you for her wisdom and courage in leading her widowed mother and younger brother to safety when political turmoil put their lives at risk. We remember Margaret for her great concern for the needy and her amazing example of inviting poor people to the castle to dine with her every evening, even washing their feet and serving them herself. We also thank you for her influence over her husband, King Malcolm, and the many churches, monasteries, hospices, and almshouses they founded together. In an age of arranged marriages where young royals were used as pawns in international relations, we appreciate the love Margaret and Malcolm developed during their long marriage, and Malcolm's receptiveness to Margaret's many innovative ideas to civilize society. Help us appreciate what we have as we share with those without means of support, for we pray in the name of the Servant King who served those in need during his ministry on earth, and whose Holy Spirit continues to comfort all of creation. Amen.

November 26

Sojourner Truth, Evangelist, Abolitionist, Women's Rights Orator, 1883

HOLY COMFORTER, we praise you for Sojourner's great faith in you, instilled by her own mother. We deplore slavery itself and the violence they and other slaves endured. We praise you for calling Sojourner out of bondage and for strengthening her in the fight against slavery and in the struggle for rights for all women. This magnificent woman's gifts for preaching and getting to the heart of the matter were unequalled. Her trust in you through years of extreme physical and emotional abuse challenges us to hold tight to you and to act, despite our fears, when we are called. We especially praise you that Sojourner had the independence of mind to ask you for an entirely new name, and that she made the most of being a strong woman, equal to, or better than, many a man. Help us claim our strengths and independence as we work with those in need. In the name of the Mother Spirit who empowered Sojourner and who empowers us, we pray. Amen.

December 1

Rosa Parks, One of the Sparks of the Civil Rights Movement in 1955, Montgomery, Alabama

LORD GOD, we praise you for your daughter, Rosa, and for her courage in refusing to give up her seat on a segregated bus. Her "small action" became one of the sparks that started the Civil Rights Movement. We thank you that this woman had the will to let her case be used to fight segregation laws in court. She worked to obtain black voting rights in Alabama and for civil rights throughout her life. When our actions have dire consequences, help us be as courageous as Rosa and her colleagues were and recall the good that ultimately came from their courage. Amen.

December 5

Phillis Wheatley, Published Poet, Founder of African-American Literature, 1784

GOD OF MERCY AND TRUTH, we praise you for this brilliant Gambian woman who learned to read and then to write poetry. Although we deplore slavery, we appreciate the opportunities she had to write and to travel to England to oversee the publication of her writing. Phillis developed African-American literature by using the white European literary models to write about her experiences in Africa and as a slave. We thank you that one of her poems was sent to George Washington and was published to encourage patriotism during the Revolutionary War. Amen.

December 7

Rosie the Riveter, 1940s

HOLY GOD, we praise you for the women, symbolized by Rosie the Riveter, who left their homes to work during World War II. They were instrumental in keeping the factories and offices of America going. They quickly learned and ably performed jobs that were vital to their country's success. Along with the contributions of these working women, we also thank you for the stability and community services provided by the women who stayed home. Amen.

December 12

Our Lady of Guadalupe

PRECIOUS MOTHER, you have made the poor of this world rich in faith through the appearances of the Lady of Guadalupe. We praise you for these miracles and for the great love she inspires. Continue to bless us as we look for you in the faces of the women and men here in our community and wherever we go in our travels. For it is in the name of Jesus we pray in thanksgiving for your gift of the Lady of Guadalupe through the power of the Holy Spirit. Amen.

December 18

U.N. Convention of the Elimination of all Forms of Discrimination against Women, 1979

MOTHERLY CREATOR, we praise you for this gathering of people from all over the world and for the hope and courage they demonstrated in calling for the elimination of all forms of discrimination against women. You know how women are treated in every corner of the earth. Locally, nationally, and globally, inspire us to affirm the steps that have been taken to eliminate discrimination against women. Bless our sisters who are discovering their potential, especially when they are in places or situations that limit them because of their sex. For we pray in the name of the God of Wholeness. Amen.

December 21

Winter Solstice

CREATOR OF THE UNIVERSE, we praise you for this, the shortest day and longest night of the year. Thank you for the beauty of light and darkness and the blending that gives dawn and dusk, daybreak and twilight. As we look forward to increasing daylight, we acknowledge the diminishing nighttime. As we go about our daily lives, remind us that we are part of your creation just as the cycle of day and night are. Whether we are morning people or night people, help us to live fully in harmony with Mother Earth. Amen.

December 23

Rabbi Abraham Heschel, **Asked God for and Received Wonder, not Success, in Life, 1972**

HOLY ONE, we bless you for Abraham and his call to link Hasidic mysticism and modern seekers. We praise you for his gift with words and his profound sense of your presence in the world. We also thank you for Abraham's courageous stands against racism, anti-Semitism, and the Viet Nam War. Grant us the courage to stand up for our convictions and to reflect your divine image as radiantly as he did. In the name of God, the Merciful and the Just. Amen.

December 25

Celebration of Jesus' Birth

MOTHERLY FATHER, we praise you for the gift of your anointed baby who was born of a woman who was as fully human as our own mothers are. Help us, we pray, to make our hearts into a welcoming, yet sturdy, manger suitable to receive this precious baby from this day forth. We lift up all the babies worldwide who are born today and their families, too. We ask you to bless them as they grow, and for the people around them to cherish them, just as Mary and Joseph cherished their newborn baby and your only begotten son. For we pray in the name of Jesus whose birth we celebrate today. Amen.

December 29

St. Melania the Younger, **Philanthropist, Founder of Churches, Convents, Monasteries, Pilgrim, 439**

GREAT CREATOR, we praise you for St. Melania the Younger's generosity and adventurous spirit. We note her role in founding churches, convents, and monasteries in Europe and the Middle East. We applaud Melania's sharing her wealth to help the poor and sick. We are amazed at this woman who managed to free some 8,000 slaves in a mere two years, and who bought off pirates when she and her followers were shipwrecked and threatened. Melania's courageous devotion in making a pilgrimage to Jerusalem and settling there are inspiring. Help us to share what we have joyously and to use our talents to benefit those in need, whether they are nearby or far away. Glory to the Open-handed One. Amen.

December 30

Josephine Butler, **Worker among Women, 1905**

HOLY JESUS, we thank you for Josephine's work for women's rights and for her vision of life as it could be. We applaud her foresight in understanding your life and work as signs of the equality between the sexes. Give us the ability to see you in our world and to continue Josephine's work so all people, regardless of their sex, come to value themselves as you do. We pray in the name of God whose Spirit empowers us to become more wholly ourselves. Amen.

December 31

Birth of the New Year

HEAVENLY CREATOR OF TIME AND SPACE, we thank you for bringing us to the close of another year. As we wait for the coming of the New Year, be with us all. Guide those who use the birth of the New Year as an excuse for playing too hard. Give them the strength and common sense to draw the line before harm is done. We praise you for those who look forward to the New Year—in an attitude of holy play—just as they would the joyous birth of a new baby. We lift up those who dread new birth of any kind. We ask that they can look through the mists of uncertainty and straight into the loving security of Jesus' face. In his name we pray. Amen.

PART FIVE

Rites, Rituals, and Services for Special Occasions

Front Porch: Services of Beginnings

Whereas the services and Collects in the previous parts may be for private or public worship, the services in Part Five are intended to be shared. On the front porch, we have two services of beginnings. One is to welcome a person into a new family. Families grow in many ways—through childbirth, fostering, adoption, re-marriage, commitments between two adults, and by hosting foreign exchange students. The second service is to join two adults into a covenant relationship. In the kitchen, there is a service to Redeem Eden's Goodness. It is an alternative form of Lord's Supper, using an apple and fresh water in lieu of the bread and wine. On the side porch are two services of transformation, one for healing and one for reconciliation. In the garden is a labyrinth service. It may be used on its own or as part of the service of reconciliation.

A RITUAL OF WELCOMING A NEW FAMILY MEMBER

The Facilitator says the parts in plain print; the community say the parts in bold print.

Greeting

As a mother caresses her long awaited new-born,
may our Motherly Father blanket creation in the tenderness of Love.

Invocation to the Spirit of Holiness

Come, holy name of the Messiah;
Come, power of grace that is from heaven;
Come, perfect compassion;
Come, exalted gift;
Come, communion of the blessing;
Come, revealer of the hidden mysteries;
Come, Mother of the seven houses whose rest is in the eighth house;
Come, messenger of reconciliation and communicate with the minds of these youngsters;
Come, Spirit of Holiness, and purify the obstacles of their hearts . . .
THE ACTS OF JUDAS THOMAS, ACT II, ¶142

The Ministry of Be-Ribboning a Teether

The Facilitator says to the community:

A threefold cord is not quickly broken.
ECCLESIASTES 4:12

Instructions to the community

Please divide yourselves up into groups of seven to nine people. The attendants are passing around baskets with ribbons and teethers. Everyone gets to choose a ribbon to tie onto the teether. Please use about a third of the ribbon to loop around the teether and knot, leaving a long tail hanging down the outside of the teether.

After everyone has finished, the godparents gather up the teether(s). While the godfather holds the teether, the godmother pulls all the tails into a bunch and loops them into a simple knot. After she does this, she holds the be-ribboned teether aloft, and prays:

Declaration of Support

Holy Trinity, Three-in-One and One-in-Three,

This teether reminds us that each and every one of us, including our Brother Jesus, came into this world as a baby. The parents gathered here remind us that you are both Mother and Father to us. The knotted ribbons remind us that, though we are each unique individuals, we are also One Body. Bind us together in our love for you and (child's name) so as s/he grows in knowledge and love, in wisdom and stature, s/he may be secure enough to take the risks you call her/him to take. When the time comes for her/him to step out in faith and maturity, enable us to support her/his parents so they may joyfully encourage their daughter/son in the path s/he has chosen. Let this be-ribboned teether be a symbol of our dependence on you and on each other. Amen.

AN ALTERNATIVE LORD'S PRAYER

Eternal Spirit,
Life-Giver, Pain-Bearer, Love-Maker
Source of all that is and that shall be,
Father and Mother of us all,
Loving God, in whom is heaven:
The hallowing of your name echo through the universe!
The way of your justice be followed by the people of the world!
Your heavenly will be done by all created beings!
Your commonwealth of peace and freedom sustain our hope, and
come on earth!
With the bread we need for today, feed us.
For the hurts we absorb from one another, forgive us.
In times of temptation and test, strengthen us.
From trials too severe to endure, spare us.
From the grip of all that is evil, free us.
For you reign in the glory of the power that is love,
now and forever. Amen.

Jim Cotter

Invocation to the Giver of Joy and Rest

Come, gift of the exalted one;
Come, perfect compassion;
Come, Holy Spirit;
Come, revealer of the mysteries of the chosen among the prophets;
Come, treasure of majesty;
Come, beloved of the compassion of the most high;
Come, silence, revealer of the mysteries of the exalted one;
Come, speaker of hidden things and pointer of the works of our God;
Holy Dove that bears twin young,
Come, hidden Mother;
Come, giver of life through her secret, and revealer through her actions;
Come, giver of joy and rest to all who join her;
Come, communicate with us . . .

The Acts of Judas Thomas, Act V, ¶50

Closing

Laugh with the Sacred Three, the Holy Trinity, the Divine Mystery, from the beginning of creation, here in the present, and on into life anew. Amen.

A RITUAL OF JOINING TWO PEOPLE INTO A COVENANT RELATIONSHIP

The Facilitator says the parts in plain print; the community say the parts in bold print.

Greeting

In sharing your love, you encourage others to risk love.
Come, love and be loved.

Invocation of the Archangels

Raphael to the east of us,
Michael to the south,
Gabriel to the west of us,
Uriel to the north.

Christ to uphold us,
God up above,
Holy Spirit to guide us
In peace, safety and love.

The Facilitator says to the community:

Set me as a seal upon your heart, as a seal upon your arm; for love is strong as death, passion fierce as the grave. Its flashes are flashes of fire, a raging flame. Many waters cannot quench love, neither can floods drown it. If one offered for love all the wealth of one's house, it would be utterly scorned.
SONG OF SOLOMON 8:6–7

Declaration of Agreement

The Facilitator asks one partner and then the other:

(Name), will you take this woman (man) to be your beloved? Will you love, respect, and care for her (him)? Will you forgive and seek forgiveness? Will you stay together in good times and in bad?

Answer

I will.

THE SPIRIT OF LOVE

I am the excitement at the thought of you.
I am the sparkle in your eyes when you look at each other.
I am the electricity in your touches, tickles, and caresses.
I am the ecstasy of intimacy.
I am the intimacy of afterglow.

When miscommunication causes tempers to flare, I am the balm
that calms the hurts.

I am the determination to work through past hurts to free you to love now and into your future.
I am also the commitment to try again when the going gets tough.
When fatigue or busy-ness stretches the relationship, I am the kindling that re-ignites the flames of love.
I am the humility that allows you to say you're sorry.
I am the graciousness that accepts an apology.

I am the Life-blood of the relationship.
Throughout your life together, I will ebb and flow like a creek meandering along its bed.
Times of drought may be followed by flash floods.
When the relationship feels dry, look to the Supreme Rain-Maker for refreshment.
When boulders or sharp jagged rocks block your way, seek out a professional Earth-mover.
When stones sparkle in the sunlight just for you two or pebbles prick your souls, share your joys and sorrows with your neighbors along the way.
For in sharing your love, you encourage others to risk love.
Go, love and be loved.

The Ministry of the Prayersticks

The Facilitator says to the community:

A threefold cord is not quickly broken.
ECCLESIASTES 4:12

Sisters and brothers, in preparation for this Joining Ritual, (Name) and (Name) and their attendants got together to make these two prayersticks, one for (Name) and one for (Name). The two prayersticks were then joined together to form this larger, sturdier prayerstick. It is an outward and visible sign of their love of God and of each other and of our support of their union.

The Joining with Handfasting

Handfasting is an ancient European tradition whereby the couple, facing each other, join their left hands together and their right hands, too. From above, the two bodies with outstretched arms and clasped hands form a figure eight, the sign for infinity, the Divine Mystery.

The Facilitator says to the couple:

(Name) and (Name), as I hold the prayerstick, clasp your left hands together around the prayerstick and also your right hands together around the prayerstick (either above or below the left hands as is comfortable).

Before we move on to the promises, I'd like you to take a moment to feel God's presence and the strength of your love.

The Promises

The Facilitator guides one partner and then the other in the promises, beginning with "repeat after me":

I, (Name), take you, (Name), to be my beloved, to live together in a covenant relationship. I love and respect you. I care for you. I will forgive you and seek forgiveness. I will stay with you in good times and in bad. This is my sincere promise.

Personalized promises may be made here.
The Facilitator stands with the community as all proclaim their support of the union.

We, the family and friends of (Name) and (Name) have witnessed the promises joining them together. This is a public celebration of the love and commitment that (Name) and (Name) have already made in private. With you, Holy Trinity, as one strand of the cord, we, their community, take our place as another strand, so that as (Name) and (Name) become one, the three-stranded cord of their union will stay strong and healthy. From this day on, we proclaim (Name) and (Name) are one. What God has joined together, let no one and nothing divide.

Exchange of Rings

The Facilitator guides one partner and then the other in the exchange of rings, beginning with "repeat after me":

(Name), I give you this ring as a sign that you are my beloved, and I am yours.

Prayers

The Facilitator prays for the newly-joined couple.

FOR THE HOME

Love-Giver, Home-Builder, bless (Name) and (Name)'s efforts to make a home that is a haven of peace and stability for them. Just as no one is an island, no couple can be, either. Help them balance their time alone with time for friends and family and times apart for individual growth. Guide them in establishing healthy boundaries around their relationship. For parents who are especially excited about gaining a new daughter or son without losing their own, remind them of the newly-joined couple's need for emotional and physical space. Give family and friends discernment in how to be supportive without being overwhelming or intrusive. As (name) and (name) leave here today, joined together as one, remind them and us that though they are one, they are also still individuals moving towards wholeness with God, their community, and creation. Amen.

AN ALTERNATIVE LORD'S PRAYER

Eternal Spirit,
Life-Giver, Pain-Bearer, Love-Maker
Source of all that is and that shall be,
Father and Mother of us all,
Loving God, in whom is heaven:
The hallowing of your name echo through the universe!
The way of your justice be followed by the people of the world!
Your heavenly will be done by all created beings!
Your commonwealth of peace and freedom sustain our hope, and
come on earth!
With the bread we need for today, feed us.
In the hurts we absorb from one another, forgive us.
In times of temptation and test, strengthen us.
From trials too severe to endure, spare us.
From the grip of all that is evil, free us.
For you reign in the glory of the power that is love,
now and forever. Amen.

JIM COTTER

Transition

Loving God, at this service marking the beginning of (Name) and (Name)'s life together, we remember other kinds of beginnings. Despite the excitement of anticipation, people beginning a new life may feel a sense of loss. We ask you to comfort those who are frightened or unsure about the way their lives are unfolding. We ask you to bless those who are beginning new lives: a baby being born or adopted, children being fostered, adopted, and those gaining a step-family, those who move from one place to another, and those who are moving from this life into the next. We especially lift up these two individuals who have committed themselves to each other to live together as a family. We praise you for the ways your light illuminates our lives during times of change. Like the leaves on a tree that drop off in the autumn only to bud and blossom again in the spring, strengthen those in transition so they can lovingly detach from their old ways of life. Help them become firmly rooted wherever you are transplanting them, so they may grow and bear fruit in their new life. For we pray in the name of Jesus who was born into this life as a baby, grew to adulthood, died as a relatively young man, yet arose to new life for our sake. **Amen.**

Closing

In sharing your love, you encourage others to risk love.
Go, love and be loved.

Kitchen

A RITE TO REDEEM EDEN'S GOODNESS

The Facilitator says the parts in plain print; the community say the parts in bold print.

Greeting

May the Light shine in you and through you,
And all around you. Amen.

O SACRED THREE

O Sacred Three, you come to us in a multiplicity of Trinities. We recall the times when you were called Virgin, Mother, Crone, and Father, Mother, Son, and finally Father, Son, and Holy Spirit. We call to you out of the depths of our minds, our souls, and these physical frames, our bodies, asking that you heal the hurts, confirm the well-being, and inspire the transcendent in our yesterdays, todays, and tomorrows. All this we ask whatever our ages, our sexual persuasions, or our place in the circle leading deeper to you, Motherly Father, dearest Brother, and Spirit of Wholeness. **Amen.**

A COLLECT FOR THE COMMEMORATION OF ST. MARY, JESUS' MOTHER, AND ST. CLARE

Holy God, we praise you for Mary and Clare, one a mother, one celibate. When faced with your call, both said yes to you, the God of love.

Whether we are called, like Mary, to be mothers, or like Clare, to be single and childless, help us live our lives lovingly and faithfully.
Empower us to say yes to your call so your love may abound in this world and the next, in the name of Jesus, Mary's son, and the power of the Holy Spirit who overshadowed Mary and empowered Clare.
Amen.

THE SAMARITAN WOMAN AS A PREACHER OF THE GOSPEL, JOHN 4:7–30, 39

Blessed are you, O woman, for you did not conceal your judgment about what you discovered. The glorious Treasury was Himself present for your need because of His love. Your love was zealous . . . to share your treasure with your city. Blessed woman, your discovery was the Discoverer of the lost.

O woman in whom I see a miracle as great as Mary! For this one brought forth His body as a baby from within her womb in Bethlehem, but you by your mouth made Him manifest as an adult in Shechem, the village of His father's household. Blessed are you, woman, who brought forth by your mouth light for those in darkness.

Mary, the thirsty land in Nazareth, conceived our Lord by her hearing. You, too, O woman thirsting for water, conceived the Son by your hearing. Blessed are your ears that drank from the Spring that gave water to the world. Mary planted Him in the manger, but you planted Him in the ears of His hearers.

Your word, O woman, became a mirror so that He would see inside your hidden heart. You had said, "Lo, the Messiah is coming, and when He comes, He will give us everything." Behold the Messiah for whom you waited, chaste woman. With your voice . . . your prophecy was fulfilled.

Your voice, O woman, brought forth fruit first with the Gospel, even before the apostles. The apostles were forbidden to proclaim Him among the Gentiles and the Samaritans. Blessed is your mouth that He opened and confirmed. The Granary of life took and gave you seeds to sow. You went into a city that was as dead as Sheol and revived your dead people.

ST. EPHREM THE SYRIAN'S *HYMNS ON VIRGINITY 23:1, 4–7*

Meditation (optional)

A Meditation may be given by anyone in the community or by an invted speaker.
The Facilitator says: Let us pray together.

O WONDROUS MOTHER

O Wondrous Mother of the universe, during the process of bringing our world to birth, you placed the sparks of cyclic creativity, death, and new life into Mother Earth and into those who populate her. Open our senses to perceive you in the tranquility of the night sky, the beauty of the sunrise, and the grandeur of the sunset. Give us such a wonder at your creation that we cherish and enjoy the earth as we would our aging magnificent mothers and grandmothers. As we draw closer to you through seeing the creative miracles of nature, nourish us so that we can go and bear a vast orchard of fruit, fruit that will last here in our community and beyond. For we pray in your name, the Sacred Place of our birth, the Nurturing Place of our dance towards death, and the Hallowed Place of new life.

Amen.

AN ALTERNATIVE LORD'S PRAYER

Eternal Spirit,
Life-Giver, Pain-Bearer, Love-Maker
Source of all that is and that shall be,
Father and Mother of us all,
Loving God, in whom is heaven:
The hallowing of your name echo through the universe!
The way of your justice be followed by the people of the world!
Your heavenly will be done by all created beings!
Your commonwealth of peace and freedom sustain our hope, and
come on earth!
With the bread we need for today, feed us.
In the hurts we absorb from one another, forgive us.
In times of temptation and test, strengthen us.
From trials too severe to endure, spare us.
From the grip of all that is evil, free us.
For you reign in the glory of the power that is love,
now and forever. Amen.

JIM COTTER

Presentation of the Offering

This includes a pitcher of water and a basket of fruit arranged so the apples are clearly visible. The pitcher and basket are to be set in the center of the table. A knife will be needed to core and slice the apple.

The Core of a Rite to Redeem Eden's Goodness

The facilitator starts the responsive affirmations.

Let's celebrate being a community moving toward wholeness through the Sacred Three.

Yes! Let's celebrate the Divine Wholeness of Creation.

Let's celebrate by reclaiming the apple as one of God's bounteous gifts to us.

Yes! Let's celebrate God's Goodness toward us.

Let's celebrate by recalling Jesus' gift of Living Water to the Samaritan woman.

Yes! Let's celebrate God's Life in us.

The facilitator continues

Let us recall our Creator's words, prior to the birth of humanity,
"Let us make humankind in our image, according to our likeness; . . .
So God created humankind in his image,
in the image of God he created them; male and female he created them. . . .
God blessed them. . . . God saw everything that he had made, and indeed, it was very good."

We reject the ancient and modern practices of blaming Eve alone for the Fall and
of identifying the fruit of the Tree of Knowledge of Good and Evil as an apple.
We re-claim the goodness of women and apples and all of creation by recalling the Scripture, "God saw all he had made, and behold, it was very good."

Further we remember the hope of our Brother's words to the Samaritan woman,
"Everyone who drinks of this water will be thirsty again,
but those who drink of the water that I will give them will never be thirsty again.
The water that I give will become in them a spring of water gushing up to eternal life."

Motherly Father, we praise you for your many gifts, especially for this apple and this water. Just as an apple grows from a seed into what you intend it to be, bless our efforts to grow in grace to become more and more the daughters and sons you desire us to be. Just as the outcast Samaritan woman joyfully spread the seed of the Gospel after your son gave her the Living Water, fill us with that Living Water, so that we, too, may spread the seeds of the Eternal Fountain of Life in our communities.

We lift up this apple and this water to you and ask you to bless them so that they may be signs of your Goodness and Life in us and in our world.
All this we ask in the name of the Anointed One, Jesus, through the power of the Holy Spirit.
Amen.

The facilitator takes an apple and slices it into pieces of any size and shape and puts them on a suitable plate. The coring and cutting of the apple is a central part of the service. When the facilitator lifts up the plate with the apple pieces, the community says:

Holy God, Creator of the universe, we praise you for giving us this apple, fruit of the earth.
It will become for us a sign of our Goodness through you.

When the facilitator takes the pitcher and pours the water into a glass, the community says:

Lord God, Creator of the universe, we praise you for giving us this water, fruit of the earth.
It will become for us a sign of your Life in us.

Instructions for passing the apple and water:
As the plate with apple pieces is passed, each person gives a piece to the next person and says:

Taste and see that you are good.

As the glass of water is passed, each person hands the glass to the next person and says:

Taste and feel the Living Water in you.

After everyone has eaten the apple of goodness and drunk the water of new life, the facilitator and community pray together:

O Creator of the Dance,
We thank you for creating us good, in your image, and for giving us new life.
We thank you for your many gifts to us past, present, and future.
We praise you that Joy is a part of your salvation,
and for the many ways it can be expressed—giggles, goose bumps, tears, and movement.
We join with you in the dance of life!

Closing

Loving God, hold us as the apple of your eye.
May your Living Water always flow through us like a river out into the world.

Side Porch: Services of Transformation

Whereas the Services of Beginning were on the front porch and A Rite to Redeem Eden's Goodness was in the heart of the banquet hall, the kitchen, the two services of transformation are tucked away in an open, yet safe place—the side porch. The Service of Healing is designed for healing on a personal or small scale, close-to-home level. The Service of Reconciliation is intended to bridge the gulfs in relationships between peoples of differing faiths as well as those with no faith.

A SERVICE OF HEALING

Preparing the Space for Worship:
Have baskets at the door with fresh flowers, so people with prayer requests may take a flower for each person or situation they wish to offer up. A table with pictures of the people or events being prayed for may be displayed in the center of the circle. The table needs to be big enough for the flowers to be placed on it during the ritual. Ask for volunteers to bring up the flowers for the petitions in the Prayers of the Community.
The Facilitator says the parts in plain print; the community say the parts in bold print.

Greeting

As a caring healer listens attentively to her patient,
listen, Heavenly Healer, to the aches of our hearts and the sighs of our souls.

Song of the Bear Matron to her Cubs: A Catechesis

Classical Greece, 2nd century B.C.E.

Teacher: Whom do we mourn?
Students: We mourn the beautiful babies
who are stillborn in death;
We mourn the handsome men
who are destroyed in war;
We mourn the rape of women
who are defenseless and afraid;
We mourn the solitary elderly
alone by their dying fire.
We mourn the destruction of the earth's greatest treasures,
leaving us depleted and anxious and tired.
Teacher: When do we mourn?
Students: We mourn in the morning;
we mourn at the noontime;
we mourn in the evening;
and in the midnight.
We mourn in the spring,
the summer, the fall.
We mourn in the winter—
then, most of all.
Teacher: Where do we mourn?
Students: We mourn in our beds;
we mourn in our chairs;
we mourn in our chores;
we mourn in our cares;
we mourn in our going;
and coming and leaving.
Our mourning is continuous,
but much more than grieving
on the outside where it's seen,
our grief must be hidden
deep down within ourselves,
disguised by our smiles.
Teacher: How do we mourn?
Students: We mourn by giving succor;
we mourn by cooking meals;
we mourn by sweeping hearthstones;
we mourn by scrubbing tiles;
we mourn by sewing and weaving;
and by birthing and dying;

by living out our sorrow;
by smiling and by lying.

Teacher: Why do we mourn?

Students: We mourn because we have to.
We mourn because we're made
to experience men's superiority,
to stand in their shade,
To be their helpmeet,
To be their spouse, or
To be their mistress.
And nothing else
is the ambition of women
who are tactful and artful,
who are inferior and weak,
who are obedient and smart,
who are docile and meek.

Teacher: Yet one other question
I would ask you my weanlings.
Look deep inside and answer with care
this one other question
that reveals what you dare—
What do we mourn?

Students: We mourn our virginity;
we mourn our liberty;
we mourn our Selves
in the dark nights of the moon.
We mourn at the hearth,
as we scatter the ashes,
and light the new flames,
for the bright nights of the moon,
and burn our cut hair in its flames.
We mourn in our homes,
which are also our prisons.
We mourn in our hearts,
which long to be free.
We mourn in our souls,
blinded from the Vision,
yearning for light and the ability to see.
We mourn our lack of virginity;
we mourn our lack of liberty;
we mourn our lack of our Selves
in the dark nights of the moon.
Until our daughters may choose to be

more than mothers and mistresses;
Until our daughters may choose to be
warriors and women with true power;
We will mourn our enslavement—
Maiden, Matron, and Crone—
in the dark nights of the moon,
in the darkest months of winter,
in the dark nights of the moon.

Teacher: Weep my daughters and be strong!

Prayers of the Community

Loving God, we join with all your saints in respect and honor for all Martyrs.
We remember
The Holy Innocents, slain by Herod,
Saint Agnes, Martyr,
Saint Perpetua and her companions, Martyrs.
Saint Francis, who was beaten by his father,

The Martyrs of the Anglican Communion,
The Martyrs of Lyons and of Europe,
The Martyrs of Uganda and Africa,
The Martyrs of Japan, Papua New Guinea, and the Pacific,
The Martyrs of North, South, and Central America,
The Martyrs of the Jewish Holocaust,
And modern day Martyrs.
O God, into your hands we commend their spirits.
Let light perpetual shine upon them.
Kindle in us hope for establishing new ways of dealing with differences.

Loving God, you who are Creator, Redeemer, and Sanctifier,
Create in your Church a spirit of compassion, especially for the violently abused,
Redeem your Church from complacency in the face of an epidemic of domestic violence, and sanctify and empower your Church in this world as a
sanctuary for all abused, violated, hurting people.
O God, heal our wounds and make us whole.

Loving God, you who are the last resort of authority,
Create a spirit of justice in our nation, our law enforcement agencies, our legal systems, especially the courts of law, for the oppressed and exploited, for the wounded and abused.

O God, have mercy on us and grant us peace.

Loving God, create in our welfare systems a sense of sympathy and understanding as well as a power to act on behalf of the fearful, the emotionally paralyzed, and the desolate.

O God, hear our cries and answer our pleas.

Loving God, create a new order in this your world in which power is measured,

not by brute force, but by gentleness and respect.

O God, hear our prayers and instill in us your Wisdom.

Loving God, we commend to you all those, especially our sisters, who suffer physically, emotionally, mentally, spiritually from domestic abuse and violence, and all those who grieve for and with them.

O God, intervene and heal.

Offer individual prayers at this time.

Loving God, we lift up to you all those, especially our sisters, who have died violent deaths as a result of domestic violence.

O God, let your eternal light shine forever on them.

Offer individual prayers at this time.

Loving God, into your hands we commend all children who live in violent homes;

provide for them advocates and guardian angels.

O God, draw the children into your loving protection and heal them.

Offer individual prayers at this time.

Loving God, we commend ourselves to you.

Make us ever mindful of our role in counteracting the violence of our world.

Empower us with your healing to reach out in love to those who suffer in silence and fear from the compulsion and secrecy of domestic violence. Release them and us from the tightening spiral of brutality.

O God, help us to see with your eyes,
hear with your ears,
feel with your heart, and
heal with your hands.

Loving God, accept these fervent prayers of your people;

in the multitude of your mercies, look with compassion upon us, and upon all who turn to you for help; for you are gracious, O Lover of souls,

and to you we give glory, now and forever. Amen.

AN ALTERNATIVE LORD'S PRAYER:

Eternal Spirit,
Life-Giver, Pain-Bearer, Love-Maker
Source of all that is and that shall be,
Father and Mother of us all.
Loving God, in whom is heaven:
The hallowing of your name echo through the universe!
The way of your justice be followed by the people of the world!
Your heavenly will be done by all created beings!
Your commonwealth of peace and freedom sustain our hope, and come on earth!
With the bread we need for today, feed us.
In the hurts we absorb from one another, forgive us.
In times of temptation and test, strengthen us.
From trials too severe to endure, spare us.
From the grip of all that is evil, free us.
For you reign in the glory of the power that is love,
now and forever. Amen.

JIM COTTER

The Flower Ritual

The Facilitator says

As you come up to put your flower(s) on the table, visualize giving the Creator of All Life whoever or whatever needs to be healed. As you put your flower on the table, you may make your request either silently or out loud. Do what feels comfortable to you. As you walk back to your seat, visualize the person or situation resting safely in God's holy hands.

The Facilitator prays

Loving God, we recall that after your crucifixion, when you appeared in your resurrected body, your hands, side, and feet still bore the scars of the violence done to you. We ask for a transformative healing of our inner selves, so even if physical signs of brutality remain on our bodies, our emotions and spirits no longer tremble at the sight. Be with us now as we offer up these flowers with their broken stems and ourselves, our sisters and brothers, with our brokenness. Amen.

The Facilitator says:

We'll use the flower's name with the following words to make our requests:
Rose (Iris, Daffodil, etc.), thank you for sharing your beauty and fragrance with us.
As you fade in this life, take my concern for (prayer request) into the Eternal Garden of Life.

Place your flowers on the table, and offer up your prayer requests.
After everyone has finished, the Facilitator prays

God of Love, we praise you for all of your gifts of Creation and for the cycle of life, death, and new life. We thank you for flowers and for their role in healing the hurts and memories of our hearts and minds, souls and bodies. We pray in the life-giving power of the Holy Spirit. Amen.

WONDERFULLY MADE

Where can I go from your spirit?
Or where can I flee from your presence?
If I ascend to heaven, you are there;
if I make my bed in Sheol, you are there.
If I take the wings of the morning and settle at the farthest limits of the sea,
even there your hand shall lead me,
and your right hand shall hold me fast.
If I say, "Surely the darkness shall cover me,
and the light around me become night,"
even the darkness is not dark to you;
the night is as bright as the day,
for darkness is as light to you.
For it was you who formed my inward parts;
You knit me together in my mother's womb.
I praise you for I am fearfully and wonderfully made.
PSALM 139:7–14A

Closing

God knit me together in my mother's womb.
I am fearfully and wonderfully made.

A SERVICE OF RECONCILIATION

Preparing the space for worship:
Mark off a circle, a spiral, or some other pattern with candles. A table with pictures of people or events being prayed for, the symbols of the various religions and figurines of the animals used in the prayers about religions and creation may be displayed.
The Facilitator says the parts in plain print; the community say the parts in bold print.

Greeting

Even the sparrow finds a home,
And the swallow a nest for herself where she may lay her young at your altars, O Lord of my hosts, my King and my God.
PSALM 84:3

Prayers for Living in Harmony with Creation

Choose the creatures whose teachings are appropriate for your community's situation.

Great Spirit of Creation,

Hear us as we thank you for all things created. We praise you for living beings like plants, trees, and animals of land, sea, and air, and for beings whose life is known primarily to you (rocks and minerals, Mother Earth, stars, and the universe itself). We also thank you for the non-physical aspects of life—energy, thunder, spirit, creativity, and dreams. We thank you for teaching us through your creation.

Blessings to you, Great Spirit.

A moment of silence may be kept after each verse.

For elk, who teaches us to pace ourselves so we have the stamina to go the whole distance and to appreciate being in community with others of our own sex;
For bear, who teaches us about healing and the value of introspection;
For moose, who teaches us to recognize when someone has used wisdom and deserves praise;
For wolf, who teaches us to live as family;
For buffalo, who teaches us to give thanks for all we have been given and for all kinds of relationships;
For opossum, who teaches us to rely on our instincts, and to use our brains to overcome obstacles;
For squirrel, who teaches us to balance planning ahead without becoming obsessed by possessions or the effort to obtain them;
For rabbit, who teaches us to find a safe place to nurture ourselves in times of uncertainty and to give up our fears;
For horse, who teaches us to balance our power and to value the journey; and
For panther, who teaches us to step gently on Mother Earth.
Blessings to you, Great Spirit, for the four-legged ones.

For spider, who teaches us about the infinite possibilities of creation and to appreciate the female energy of the creative force.
Blessings to you, Great Spirit, for the creepy-crawlers.

For eagle, who teaches us to soar above the mundane to communicate with Spirit;
For hawk, who teaches us to observe the messages life sends us; and
For swan, who teaches us to surrender to your power, to accept the healing and transformation of our lives, and to re-connect with Mother Earth.
Blessings to you, Great Spirit, for the greater winged ones.

For dragonfly, who teaches us to see through the illusion of reality and to face change willingly.
Blessings to you, Great Spirit, for the little winged ones.

For otter, who teaches us to play; and
For dolphin, who teaches us about the sacred breath of life and how to communicate with the rhythms of nature.
Blessings to you, Great Spirit, for the water creatures.

For snake, who teaches us about the energy of wholeness and cosmic consciousness and that all things in creation are equal.
Blessings to you, Great Spirit, for the no-legged ones.

May these prayers of thanksgiving enable us to respect all of creation so we humans may live in harmony with you and your world. For we pray in the spirit of creative harmony. **Amen.**

May all creation be showered with the essence of your Divine Beauty,
So healing and reconciliation may abound.

AL-'ASMA' AL-HUSNA, "THE BEAUTIFUL NAMES"

Holy One of One-Hundred Names,
three of which are Compassion, Love, and Mercy,
We acknowledge our offenses against you and your creation.
In our attempts to be holy, too often we have listened to others
instead of trusting our own God-given instincts.
We have accepted distorted images of women for so long
that we no longer recognize the godly goodness of our own voices.
We have tarnished the unique God-shaped image that you so tenderly created inside each one of us,
female and male.
We confess that, at times, we have not loved you or our neighbors;
We have not loved ourselves nor have we loved Creation.
We are rarely able to receive your all-encompassing love.
Instead of fanning the flames of your love in our midst,
too often we have quenched the divine sparks.
Instead of allowing your Holy Breath to swirl around us freely, sometimes
we have tried to trap the breeze in a box to be used for our purposes.
We ask you to blow away the cobwebs of temptation and to blot out the stain of our offenses.
We pray that your light may shine through us, and we may be all you created us to be.

We hope that we may reflect your Glorious Harmony in the world.
We ask this in your many names, O God of One Hundred Names,
but especially in the name of Jesus through the power of the Holy Spirit.
Amen.

If A Labyrinth Service is to be part of the Service of Reconciliation, you may insert it here.

In the words of Desmond Tutu, "I am human because I belong,"
we pray for the peoples of the world, their faith traditions, and those with no religion.

Prayers for the followers of the religions of the world and for those with no religion

Gracious Spirit, we offer these petitions for reconciliation of the peoples of the world, acknowledging the wealth of religious diversity and cultures in our global community. We pray also for our friends, relatives, and those who claim no religion. Draw near to each and every one.

With each petition (plain print), walk into the spiral (or one way around the circle). Visualize offering the Luminous One the relationships that need reconciliation.
With each response (bold print), walk out of the spiral (or the other way around the circle). Visualize a world where people of different religions and people of no religion are living in harmony, reconciled to one another, to creation, and to the Holy Mystery.

In the knowledge that aspects of any religion may be taken to extremes, we pray for those whose human dignity has been diminished because of someone else's understanding of religion.
Matka Mother, have mercy.
We pray for those whose faith has been shaken by extremists of any kind.
Pendo Love, have mercy.
We pray especially for those living in areas of religious conflict.
Sakina Presence, have mercy.
We pray also for those who have used their faith to justify abuse of the earth.
Tz'u Compassion, have mercy.
We admit that, at times, we diminish the Divine Spark within through our own misundertanding of Love.
Esperanza Hope, have mercy.

Matka, Pendo, Sakina, Tz'u, Esperanza, whether we pray in Czech, Swahili, Arabic, Chinese, or Spanish, we seek you who are Mother, Love, Presence, Compassion, and Hope. We ask for forgiveness for our part in tarnishing the Divine Image. Through these petitions, we hope for reconciliation in any relationships that have become strained or shattered through the misuse of a religious belief, practice, or tradition. Be with us now as we celebrate the potential for Goodness that is unique in each faith. We also lift up those who have no faith or religion and respect their integrity.

We lift up those who follow the faiths that arose out of the Middle East: Judaism, Christianity, Islam, Zoroastrianism, and the Baha'i Faith.

Reader 1: Most especially we thank you for Judaism's belief in One God and the gift of the Torah, the core of which is, according to Micah 6:8, "to do justice, and to love kindness, and to walk humbly with your God,"

Reader 2: for Christianity's emphasis on God as Trinity and Jesus' teachings, the core of which is to love God and to love one's neighbor;

Reader 3: for Islam's belief in submission to Allah (The God) and its emphasis on love, forgiveness, and generosity to others as demonstrated by the prophet Muhammad;

Reader 4: for Zoroastrianism's emphasis on personal responsibility, the worship of Ahura Mazda as the source of all that is good, the renunciation of evil, and for the prophet Zarathustra;

Reader 5: and for the Baha'i Faith's emphasis on the spiritual unity of mankind, peace and universal education, and, especially, its affirmation of the equality of women and men.

Procession with the Parasol of Paradise

A volunteer processes joyfully around the room with the parasol(s) the community made. Worshippers may throw flower petals or confetti at the parasol to signify God's blessings. When the parasol is returned to it stand, the worshippers proclaim:

Glory to you, All-Seeing One.

We lift up those who follow the faiths that grew out of South Asia: Buddhism, Jainism, Hinduism, and Sikhism.

Reader 1: Most especially we thank you for Buddhism's emphasis on being Awake and The Middle Way between the extremes of asceticism and self-indulgence;

Reader 2: for Jainism's emphasis on liberating the soul and the doctrine of the many-sidedness of reality which allows for religious and political tolerance;

Reader 3: for Hinduism's belief that other religions are alternate paths to the eternal Truth (God);

Reader 4: and for Sikhism's beginning as a religion of reconciliation between Hinduism and Islam, and for its emphasis on worshipping the True Name.

Procession with the Parasol of Paradise

See page 179 for instructions.

Glory to you, All-Seeing One.

We lift up those who follow the faiths that developed in East Asia: Taoism, Confucianism, and Shintoism.

Reader 1: Most especially we thank you for Taoism's emphasis on the inner transformation of a person from which a good society and behavior flow;

Reader 2: for Confucianism's emphasis on the virtues of filial piety, kindness, righteousness, propriety, intelligence, and faithfulness;

Reader 3: and for Shintoism's emphasis on gratitude for the blessings of the kami (spirits) and the ancestors.

Procession with the Parasol of Paradise

See page 179 for instructions.

Glory to you, All-Seeing One.

We lift up those who follow the faiths based on oral traditions that have been passed down in many places of the Earth.

Reader 1: Most especially we thank you for Native American Traditions and their making us conscious of our intimate relationship to the whole of creation—mineral, plant, animal, and human;

Reader 2: for the Oral Traditions of Africa, Australia, Southeast Asia, the Pacific islands, Siberia, and South America and their emphases on maintaining personal, social, and cosmic harmony;

Reader 3: and for Wicca's emphasis on using power to change existing circumstances through interior transformation, provided no harm is done.

Procession with the Parasol of Paradise

See page 179 for instructions.

Glory to you, All-Seeing One.

We lift up those in different places of the Earth who have no beliefs in a Higher Power or Divine Being.

Reader 1: Most especially, we remember those who have never had a spiritual encounter;

Reader 2: those who have wrestled with questions or doubts, within or outside of their faith tradition;

Reader 3: those who have lost their faith altogether; and

Reader 4: those for whom a Divine Being seems unnecessary.

Procession with the Parasol of Paradise

See page 179 for instructions.

Peace be upon us all.

We praise you that so many religions have some form of the Golden Rule so there are ethical guidelines for relationships.

Gracious God, we thank you.

We praise you for calling up mystics and teachers of wisdom in the various religions to balance legalism when it arises.

Gracious God, we thank you.

We praise you that religions may be like prisms that refract Divine Light into many colors and shapes.

Gracious God, we thank you.

We praise you that most secular humanists and philosophers advocate ethical ways of living.

Gracious God, we thank you.

May these prayers of healing and thanksgiving for the peoples of the world and their many diverse religions, as well as the prayers for those without faith, bring healing and reconciliation where it is needed and build bridges between peoples, regardless of their faith experiences. For we pray in the name of all that is holy. **Amen.**

BEAUTY WAY CHANT

In beauty I walk
In beauty I walk
In beauty I walk
To the East.

In beauty I walk
In beauty I walk
In beauty I walk
To the South.

In beauty I walk
In beauty I walk
In beauty I walk
To the West.

In beauty I walk
In beauty I walk
In beauty I walk
To the North.

In beauty I walk
In beauty I walk
In beauty I walk
Up above.

In beauty I walk
In beauty I walk
In beauty I walk
Down below.

In beauty I walk
In beauty I walk
In beauty I walk
My path now.

In beauty I walk
In beauty I walk
In beauty I walk
My path now.

Garden

From the Side Porch, we leave the Banquet Hall altogether to retire to the garden in the center of which is a labyrinth, a place of centering and depth.

A LABYRINTH SERVICE

Appropriate for an Earth Day celebration.
All participants gather outside the labyrinth; the presider faces the congregation.
Drummers may provide musical accompaniment as the congregation gathers. Suggested hymn: "Many and Great" (The Dakota Hymn) from the Episcopal Hymnal *#385.*

Jesus said, "Come to me all you who are burdened and I will give you rest."
He is our Rock and our sure Foundation on whom we rest our hope.

He is the one who was once rejected.
He has become the cornerstone of our faith.

You are the royal priesthood who shares with him the care of souls in charity.
We come carrying with us our own cares and those of the people we serve.

Enter this sacred place, and journey to the One who makes all burdens light.
We come cherishing our joys and those of them whom we serve.

Enter this sacred place, and journey to the One in whom perfect joy resides.
We come seeking our own healing and the healing of those whom we serve.

Enter this sacred place, and journey to the One who was, who is, who is to be, the Living Source of all healing, health, wholeness, and holiness.
We come gladly seeking the Living Source of Life itself.

Loving God, you whose fingers spread the mountains and prairies, the rivers and oceans, the deserts and forests, you who send the rain and the wind, the dust storm and the flood, the drought and the blizzard; you who created the far-flung stars and planets, constellations and meteors, sun and moon, we, the children you made from the very stars themselves come to you, to thank you for the awesome beauty of your creation, this beautiful Mother Earth, our home.

Loving God, as season follows season, so our love of you is planted, watered, nurtured, and harvested to return to seed again and again in endless celebration of your love for us.

The congregation moves to the entrance of the labyrinth. Suggested hymn: the gospel song, "Precious Lord, Take My Hand" (by Tommy Dorsey; available online through numerous search engines) or "How Lovely is Thy Dwelling Place," from the Episcopal Hymnal *#517.*

Jesus said, "Let the children come to me."
With thanksgiving we come as children to this place of charity and healing, this place of joy and love, this place of rest and renewal. We come as chicks to the sheltering wing of the Mother.
Let us enter into the presence of our Loving God with joyful praise.

The presider, moving to the center of the labyrinth, leads the people forward, filling the labyrinth. Suggested hymns: the American spirituals "Come and Go with Me to That Land" or "I Am a Poor Wayfaring Stranger" (both available online through numerous search engines or in Lift Every Voice and Sing: An African American Hymnal, *or* Lead Me, Guide Me: The African American Catholic Hymnal) *or, "I Want to Walk as a Child of the Light," the* Episcopal Hymnal *#490.*

Wisdom has built her a house, a home of knowledge and of understanding, a place of shelter in the eaves of the Temple of God.
As a wayfarer longs for sanctuary in the storm, so do we long for the Wisdom of God.
Find rest, weary pilgrims, in this house built on the Rock.

Drummers lead an alleluia. Suggested hymn: "The Muskogee Hallelujah" from Music for Liturgy *published by St. Gregory of Nyssa Episcopal Church, San Francisco, California.*

God of Wisdom, you make this labyrinth a place of rest and reflection, of knowledge and understanding, of awareness and mindfulness.
Reveal your Wisdom to us, O Loving God. We wander in our darkness and need your Light to illumine our path.

You shower on us your Wisdom like rain on a parched land.
You bring us to flower in your season like wildflowers in the spring.
You tend us like grapevines and harvest the fruit that we willingly give to you.
May we all flourish like the crops in a good season.
You have provided abundantly for us, and from your own bounty we return our gifts to you.

Jesus our brother frequently left his disciples and went off into the wilderness to pray. May this labyrinth be to you who visit a place of solace and rest.
May this labyrinth be a place of tranquility and harmony.

The following sentences may be used for a dedication service. For a service in an already dedicated labyrinth, continue with the congregational responses.

Jesus said, "Build your house upon the rock, not the sand."
Many skillful hands worked to create this labyrinth—
Those who planned and built the labyrinth,
Those who landscaped and decorated the labyrinth, and
Those who have pledged to maintain the labyrinth.
May your labor not be in vain; may your labor be fruitful for us all.
We bless the hands that have made and will maintain this labyrinth for all to visit.

Jesus our brother on the night before his Crucifixion withdrew to a Garden to pray.
May you who walk in this labyrinth meet the Living Presence of our Brother, the Christ.
Jesus our brother, Christ our Brother, stay by our side and teach us to pray.

Say An Alternative Lord's Prayer or sing a traditional version

Eternal Spirit,
Earth-Maker, Pain-Bearer, Life-Giver,
Source of all that is and that shall be,
Father and Mother of us all.
Loving God, in whom is heaven:

The hallowing of your name echo through the universe!
The way of your justice be followed by the people of the world!
Your heavenly will be done by all created beings!
Your commonwealth of peace and freedom sustain our hope, and
 come on earth!
With the bread we need for today, feed us.
In the hurts we absorb from one another, forgive us.
In times of temptation and test, strengthen us.
From trials too severe to endure, spare us.
From the grip of all that is evil, free us.
For you reign in the glory of the power that is love,
now and forever. Amen.

JIM COTTER

Loving God, we send voices of thankful praise to you who have brought us to this time and to this labyrinth. Thank you not only for the hands that have made this labyrinth and the hands that maintain this labyrinth, but thank you also for blessing the feet that walk this labyrinth. We pray that you, our Great Companion, lift and make light the burdens of those who are heavy-laden; that you, our Great Friend, protect those who come rejoicing to this labyrinth in their happiness; that you, our Great Healer, heal all our wounds and restore us to your health, wholeness, and holiness, so that we may return from our spiritual journey to the center back into our own world renewed and strengthened to do the work you call us to do in the Name of God the Father and God the Mother, in the Name of Jesus Christ our Brother, in the Name of the Great Holy Spirit.

Amen.

Brothers and Sisters, travel in peace to the Center of this Labyrinth, rest awhile in God's grace and love, and return to your world refreshed!

Alleluia! Alleluia!

The presider leaves the center of the labyrinth accompanied by drumming. Suggested Hymn: "Jerusalem My Happy Home," the Episcopal Hymnal #620 *or "Glory, Glory, Hallelujah" in* Lift Every Voice and Sing *or* Lead Me, Guide Me.

PART SIX

About What's Inside

Chest of Drawers in Closet

One of the tidbits in the Guidelines for Readers way back at the beginning was that you're welcome to look into the closet of this banquet hall, and even into the chest of drawers. This chest is like the family chest that holds the mementos of childhood and bits of family history. The contents of some of these drawers are like the photos of a huge family reunion. You'll never be close to everyone in the picture, but it's still nice to have them properly identified. Perhaps familiarity with the names will help at the next family gathering. Some of the drawers hold treasures. These will help you expand your horizons and provide tangible access to the Divine.

Top Drawer

CRAFTS FOR USE DURING THE RITES, RITUALS, AND SERVICES

Crafts bring prayers to life by expressing the concepts and feelings physically. The preparation itself begins the prayer for the service.

To Be-Ribbon a Teether for a Ritual of Welcoming

Supplies/Preparation: basket(s); ribbons, 1/8 inch wide, variety of colors, choose ribbons that tie easily (grosgrain or lacy ribbons don't work as well); scissors to cut the ribbon; teethers.

Instructions: Choose the number of teethers depending on the number of people expected to join in the ribbon tying. Allow one teether for every seven to nine people. Cut the ribbon into sections about an arm's length (18 to 24 inches). Designate enough Godmothers and Godfathers to help with the tying of the tails during the Declaration of Support.

To Make Prayersticks for a Ritual of Joining

Supplies/Prepartion: The following supplies may be purchased in a hobby supply store: dowel rod (1/4 inch by 36 inches), acrylic paints, paint brush, one yard of leather lacing, one wooden bead large enough to contain a double width of the leather lacing, feathers, and pony beads. Larger doweling rods may be used if preferred, and 36 inches, the usual doweling rod length, is only approximate; the rod should be long enough to stick into the ground and stay standing with the painted portion being approximately 2/3 of the total length of the rod. Any color combination may be used, since this is an individual prayerstick, but the frequently used colors are listed here. There are tribal variations for the colors, so there will not be 100 percent agreement on the directional associations for the colors.

Yellow is associated with the east, spring, childhood, sprouting, and new beginnings of projects, events, programs, etc.
Red is associated with the south, summer, adolescence, growing, and the processing of projects, events, programs, etc.
Black is associated with the west, autumn, adulthood, harvesting, and the ending of projects, events, programs, etc.
White is associated with the north, winter, old age, fallow time, and the give-away of projects, events, programs, etc.

Green is associated with Mother Earth.
Blue is associated with Father Sky.

I like to paint my prayersticks in the following way: about one-fourth of the top part of the doweling rod is painted blue; then I alternate stripes of paint around the rod in the pattern of the directions: yellow, red, black, white, black, red, yellow. In this case the white would be a double width and the emphasis would be on associations with the north. Other combinations emphasizing the other directions are definitely possible.

If I were painting a prayerstick for a child I would paint the stripes in the following way: red, black, white, yellow, white, black, red with the yellow being an emphasized double width. But this is simply a suggestion; any ordering of the colors is acceptable. Then, the bottom portion of the doweling rod is painted green, usually this portion on my prayersticks is longer than the blue, but any length is possible.

None of the colors are obligatory—personal associations are definitely in order.

The next step after painting the prayerstick is to attach the leather lacing to the stick above or below the stripes with the wooden bead. I like to attach the bead so that the ends of the lacing hang equally. After attaching the lacing, but before snugging the bead to the stick, insert a feather or feathers of preferred color or colors between the stick and the beaded lacing so that the feathers are held in place, after snugging the bead tightly to the stick. Again, I would choose yellow feathers if the prayerstick were for a child, or a combination of yellow and blue for the child and the flight through Father Sky, if the prayers were for a child flying by himself or herself to visit relatives. Next, take a pony bead or beads of preferred colors and slip them onto one end of the loose lacing; then, put the quill end of a feather or two touching the top pony bead and parallel to the lacing. Finally, snug the pony bead or beads over the feathers so that the feathers are attached to the loose end of the lacing approximately two or three inches from the ends of the lacing. Repeat for the other lacing loose end.

Take the finished prayerstick and insert the unpainted end (approximately one-third of the total length of the entire stick) into the ground wherever you wish. Smudge the stick with sage, and say appropriate prayers. As long as the stick stands, or as long as the feathers still exist on the stick, your prayers will be taken to Great Spirit.

Feel free to experiment! Here is the way I made a prayerstick for my son and daughter-in-law when they got married: I painted two prayersticks with a double stripe of red to emphasize their love. Then, I attached white lacing with red feathers and red and white pony beads to emphasize the importance of using wisdom in making a marriage. I have seen beautiful marriage prayersticks made only of white and red. The marriage prayersticks usually are two prayersticks with one lacing attached to both to symbolize the couple making one marriage. Prayersticks for newborns can be painted in pastel colors and are a lovely gift to welcome the new baby. Prayersticks for teenagers leaving for college can even be painted in the school's colors! Have fun—after all, this is Holy Play!

To Make a Parasol of Paradise for a Service of Reconciliation

This service calls for a Parasol of Paradise. This parasol is loosely modeled on the exquisitely decorated umbrellas used by Christians in Ethiopia, Indonesia, and India. They are also used in the U.S. by some churches on festival days like Palm Sunday, Easter, and Pentecost, usually in a procession. The worshippers throw rose petals, or confetti, towards the umbrella. Yes, it's messy. But then, isn't life? Since parasols have largely gone out of fashion except for small ones for dolls, the Parasol of Paradise will have to be improvised. You may make your own, preferably in a group of friends, by choosing a full-size umbrella with a long handle. Umbrellas with a point or raised centerpiece in the top are easier to work with. A golf umbrella may feel too closed in for the purpose of this service.

Now the fun part: decorating the parasol of paradise! There are a number of ways to do this, depending on what kind of umbrella you have. If you like the fabric and color of the umbrella you've got, just decorate the edges, from spoke to spoke. Ribbon, fancy shoelaces, paper streamers, or strings of brightly colored beads or shells make good accents. My favorites are the shiny "'mirror'" beads. They come in all sorts of shapes. Stickers may also be used to add some color to a plain umbrella.

To change the color and the feel of a standard umbrella, drape a suitably exciting fabric over the umbrella (this is why the center top needs some sort of protrusion, to anchor the fabric). Secure the fabric to the spokes at the edges to give more stability to the parasol. Although the umbrella frame is somewhat flexible, the easiest way to do this is to take some sturdy thread, such as the thread used for quilting or beading, and hand sew the material around the spoke.

Another option is to buy a cheap umbrella with an attractive handle. Then cut the plain fabric off of the spokes and replace it with your own exquisite material. When choosing material for this project, remember that both sides of the fabric need to be attractive because the underside is clearly visible. Or, you may sew a light-weight fabric directly onto the top cloth, as if you were making a quilt. This opens up the possibility of using some of the many beautiful fabrics available, and both sides of the umbrella will be glorious.

Drawer Two

TABLE OF ANIMALS, PLANTS, AND MINERALS IN THE WEEKLY COLLECTS

The qualities or attributes and the animal correspondences in the table are taken from either Jamie Sams's *Medicine Cards* or from Ted Andrews's *Animal Speak*. Plant and mineral correspondences from several sources were matched with the qualities.

Some plants and minerals have such similar meanings to those of the animals that no additional quality was provided for them in the table. But when the meaning of a plant or mineral was used to counterbalance or enhance the animal's quality, especially if the associations were not synonymous, the appropriate meanings associated with the plant and/or mineral have been included in the table to indicate when a secondary quality is being used. By combining animal, plant, and mineral, the human praying at an altar supplies the fourth part of the four-part Order of Creation found in most Native American cosmologies. The correspondences for the animals reflect Sams's and Andrews's Eastern Woodlands (Iroquois, Choctaw, and Cherokee) backgrounds, whereas the plant and mineral correspondences are very eclectic, or pan-tribal, in origin. This means that the whole list reflects a number of different Native American traditions, not one in particular. A personal altar may be created by laying down a square yard cloth (the altar cloth may be smaller if desired, but probably should be at least one foot square). On top of the cloth place a yellow ribbon one-fourth to one-half inch in width and long enough to reach the edge of the cloth and hang over (if on a table) or extend beyond the cloth (if the altar is set up on the ground); it should be aligned east and west (standing for the East). Then, place a red ribbon aligned south and north (standing for the South), a black ribbon aligned west and east (standing for the West), and a white ribbon aligned north and south (standing for the North) on the cloth. The ribbons should overlap in the center of the cloth, forming a cross in the middle of the altar. Place a representative of the animal on the altar; the representative may be a picture or a figurine or a part of a real animal (a feather, for example). Put a vase with the flower or plant or put its fruit on the altar, in addition to a specimen of the mineral. Placing a candle in the center of the altar where the ribbons join and form a cross is also a nice touch. The altar then becomes a focus for meditation and prayer.

QUALITY	WEEK NO. AND ANIMAL	PLANT	MINERAL
Abundance	32 Buffalo	Potato Benevolence	Green Tourmaline
Action-taking	28 Antelope	Thyme	Onyx Courage
Assertiveness	42 Badger	St. John's Wort Animosity	Black Tourmaline Works against bad decisions
Boundary-making	23 Armadillo	Morning Glory Bonds	Hematite Balance priorities
Building	5 Beaver	Red Clover Industry	Abalone Balance
Camouflage	30 Fox	Coriander Hidden worth	Alexandrite Chameleon color changes
Cleansing	21 Frog	Sage	Rutilated Quartz Helps access thoughts that are source of disorder
Confrontational confidence	16 Wild Boar	Fig Argument	Obsidian Protects against abuse
Dreaming	18 Lizard	Lupine	Jasper Grounds while traveling outside the body
Fear-defeating	24 Rabbit	Amaryllis Timidity	Aquamarine Works against fear
Gathering	33 Squirrel	Corn Riches	Gold Wealth
Gentleness	36 Deer	Baby's Breath	Blue Quartz Stepping out on faith
Give-away	34 Turkey	Orange Tree Generosity	Bloodstone Martyrdom
Grace	37 Swan	Yellow Jasmine	Jade Unconditional love; aids realizing dreams
Hunting	29 Weasel	Forsythia Anticipation	Rhodonite Promotes calmness and self-assuredness; dispels anxiety

QUALITY	WEEK NO. AND ANIMAL	PLANT	MINERAL
Illusion-interpretation	17 Dragonfly	Peach Divination	Platinum Improves interpretation of psychic experiences
Independence	44 Cat	Live Oak	Chrysoprase Acceptance; non-judgemental; recognition of equality
Integration	9 Alligator	Angelica Inspiration	Moonstone
Integrity	10 Jaguar	Pine Hope in adversity	Amethyst Intuition; aids mind and spirit to work in one body
Introspection	22 Bear	Flowering Fern	Labradorite
Joy	51 Hummingbird	Wood Sorrel	Citrine
Lawfulness	47 Crow	Dandelion Oracle	Silver Aids in arbitration
Leadership	45 Mountain Lion	Scotch Fir Elevation	Topaz
Loyalty	46 Dog	Bluebell Constancy	Malachite
Magic-making	19 Raven	Holly Foresight, enchantment	Opal
Messenger	7 Hawk	Iris	Lapis Lazuli Aids opening to receive message
Migration	8 Snow Goose	Palm Resurrection	Rhodochrosite Aids against emotional and physical abuse; aids in deserving honor and respect
Mystery	20 Black Panther	Walnut Sacred sight	Fluorite Increases ability to perceive at higher levels
Nurturance	35 Turtle	Pineapple Hospitality	Smoky Quartz Attracts support

(contined on page 196)

QUALITY	WEEK NO. AND ANIMAL	PLANT	MINERAL
Patience	4 Ant	Daffodil	Herkimer Diamond Used to grid area for energy pockets
Persistence	41 Blue Jay	Water Willow	Aventurine Self-trust
Playfulness	50 Otter	Parsley Festivity	Peridot Happiness
Power	39 Horse	Mistletoe Surmount difficulty	Pearl
Protection	25 Raccoon	Juniper	Turquoise
Rebirth	3 Bat	Lily of the Valley	Sodalite Grounding at beginnings; carrying through to the end
Recreation	49 Opossum	Hyacinth Sport, game, play	Sugalite Helps spread love and light
Respect	43 Skunk	Date Righteouness	Tiger Eye Commitment
Sacred Dance	52 Grouse	Yellow Lily Gaiety	Amazonite Gentle power; order out of chaos
Scrutiny	15 Mouse	Ivy Assiduous to please	Copper Amplifies and conducts
Secret-discerning	13 Lynx	Red Rose	Clear Quartz Amplification
Self-esteem	40 Moose	Strawberry	Moss Agate
Self-protection	26 Porcupine	Mountain Ash	Carnelian Aligns, attunes inner self, opens heart
Sharing	31 Owl	White Cherry Winter	Emerald Regeneration
Spirit	12 Eagle	Sweetgrass	Sapphire
Stamina	27 Elk	Cedar Strength	Selenite/Gypsum Strength and flexibility

QUALITY	WEEK NO. AND ANIMAL	PLANT	MINERAL
Teacher	38 Wolf	Olive Tree Rabbi/Imam	Coral Aids conversation with inner mystic, brings past masters to current issues
Tradition	48 Whale	Magnolia	Diamond
Transformation	2 Butterfly	Marigold	Fire Agate Healing, balancing, transforming
Transmutation	1 Snake	Aloe Vera	Moldavite Transforms negative energy
Trickster (humorous teachings)	14 Coyote	Sycamore Curiosity	Pyrite Aids in seeing behind facades; rids depression, anxiety, false hope and danger
Weaving	6 Spider	Hollyhock Fecundity	Garnet Fertility
Wisdom	11 Salmon	Mulberry	Ruby

Drawer Three

TABLE OF THE RELIGIONS OF THE WORLD IN THE SERVICE OF RECONCILIATION

Just to be clear, the inclusion of a particular component group on this table does not mean every aspect of the group or of these religions is woman-friendly. The information on this table may be used to stimulate discussion and further study. It may also supplement the Service of Reconciliation, since the prayers in the service are necessarily short. The room in which the service takes place could have a display with this information or books on different religions to set the stage. Knowledge builds understanding, so it is a key to living in harmony with one another. For some people, visual images, like the religious symbols, may bring the prayers to life in a tangible way. When it comes to setting up your worship space, let your imagination go!

RELIGION	DATE AND PLACE OF ORIGIN	BASIC BELIEFS	FOUNDER/ CENTRAL LEADER	HOLY WRITINGS/ SOURCES	COMPONENT GROUPS
Baha'i 	1860s, Mid East	Spiritual unity, peace, universal education, equality of sexes	Bha'u'llah a.k.a. Mirza Husayn 'ali Nuri	*Most Holy Book, Hidden Words, Seven Valleys, Book of Certitude,* many others	
Buddhism 	Before 480 B.C.E., S. Asia (Nepal, near Indian border)	Philosophy, being Awake and The Middle Way between asceticism and self-indulgence	The Buddha (Siddhartha Gautama)	*Pali Tripitaka, Suttapitaka, Vinayapitaka,* and others	Theraveda, Mahayana, Tibetan
Christianity 	8–4 B.C.E., Mid East	Life, teachings, death, and resurrection of Jesus Christ	Jesus (Yeshua Bar Miryam or Yeshua Ben Yusef)	The Bible	Anglican, Catholic, Non-denominational, Orthodox, Protestant
Confucianism 	c. 500 B.C.E., E. Asia (Lu, China)	5 virtues of filial piety, kindness, righteousness, propriety, intelligence, and faithfulness	K'ung Fu-tzu (Confucius) and successors	*The Five Classics* (includes *I Ching* and *The Four Books*)	School of Principle, School of Mind

(contined on page 200)

RELIGION	DATE AND PLACE OF ORIGIN	BASIC BELIEFS	FOUNDER/ CENTRAL LEADER	HOLY WRITINGS/ SOURCES	COMPONENT GROUPS
Hinduism 	Over 10,000 Yrs. Ago, S. Asia (N. W. India)	One eternal being and truth, accepts other religions as paths to the eternal truth (God)	No one person	*Vedas, Brahamanas, Aranyakas, Upanishads, Puranas, Mahabharata, Ramayana*	Vedic (scriptural), Brahmanic (societal), Bhakti (devotional)
Islam 	622, Mid East	Submit to Allah, prophet Muhammad's love, generosity and forgiveness emphasized	Muhammad	*Quran*	Shi'as, Sunnis, Wahhabis, Sufis
Jainism 	c. 589 B.C.E., S. Asia (N. E. India)	Liberating soul, religious and political tolerance, non-violence	Mahavira, 24th and last tirthankara	*Kalpa Sutra, Dashavaikalika Sutra*	Digembaras, Shvetambaras
Judaism 	c. 722 B.C.E., Mid East	One God, the Torah and the Land of Israel	Abraham	TaNaK, Talmud, Responsa, Kabbalah, Zohar, open canon	Orthodox, Reform, Conservative, Liberal

RELIGION	DATE AND PLACE OF ORIGIN	BASIC BELIEFS	FOUNDER/ CENTRAL LEADER	HOLY WRITINGS/ SOURCES	COMPONENT GROUPS
Native American 	Prehistory, N. America, Central America, and S. America	Make us conscious of our intimate relationship to the whole of creation—mineral, plant, animal, and human		Oral traditions	Numerous tribes
Oral Traditions 	Prehistory, Africa, Australia, S.E. Asia, Pacific Islands, Siberia, S. America	Emphasize maintaining personal, social, and cosmic harmony		Oral traditions	Numerous tribes
Shintoism 	Prehistoric, E. Asia (Japan)	Gratitude for the blessings of the kami (spirits) and veneration of the ancestors	The *kami,* "spirits"	None; the earliest records are the *Kojiki* and *Nihongi.*	State Shinto, Shrine Shinto
Sikhism 	c. 1469, S. Asia (N. India)	Reconciliation of Hinduism and Islam, emphasizes worship of the True Name	Guru Nanak	*Granth Sahib (Adi Granth)*	Blends Bhakti Hinduism and Muslim Sufism

(contined on page 202)

RELIGION	DATE AND PLACE OF ORIGIN	BASIC BELIEFS	FOUNDER/ CENTRAL LEADER	HOLY WRITINGS/ SOURCES	COMPONENT GROUPS
Taoism 	From 6th–4th–3rd B.C.E., E. Asia	Inner transformation of a person from which a good society and behavior flows	Lao Tzu	*Tao Te Ching, Chuang Tzu,* and 1200 other volumes	Philosophical (tao-chia), Religious (tao-chiao), Blend of both
Wicca 	1800s, Britain, revival of pre-Christian N. Europe practices	An ye harm none, do as ye will. Use power to change circumstances by interior transformation	Many modern revivers		Many independent groups
Zoroastrianism 	1200 B.C.E., Mid East, N.E. Iran	Personal responsibility, worship of Ahura Mazda, Zarathustra as prophet and renunciation of evil	Zarathustra	*17 Gathas* in the *Yasna,* The Avesta	

Drawer Four

TABLE OF ORIGINAL WORKS BY JANE RICHARDSON JENSEN AND PATRICIA HARRIS-WATKINS

From Part One

Jane wrote these:

The daily Collects for Morning, Midday, and Evening Prayer
[The unattributed] Greetings and Closings for the services above
Song of Bast
"The Beautiful Names"
Song of Peter's Mother-in-law
Song of the Star of the East
Song of the Faces of God
Song of the Endangered
For Love's Sake
Song of Arianrhod
Song of Dark Places
Song of Time
Song of Anna
Song of She-Who-Beholds-the-Beauty-of-Her-Lord
Song of She-Who-Beats-the-Rhythm
Song of Thunder
Song of the Extinct
Song of Freya
Song of Lilith
In Praise of Relationships
Song of the Trees
Song of the Phillipian Slave Girl

Patricia wrote these:

Joyful Light
Song of White Buffalo Calf Woman
Bear Cave
Song of Changing Woman
Song for Earth Day: Pele Speaks
Song of Spider Woman

From Part Two

Patricia researched and wrote all of Part Two:

The associations and sequences of Animals, Plants, Minerals
The Fifty-Two Weekly Collects

From Part Three

Jane wrote these:

For Hope for a Parent of Teenagers
For a Mother in Distress: Parts 1, 2
For Moving (new job/military/university/ministry)
For Continuity and Connection
In Praise of Grandmothers
In Praise of Rough Diamonds
On Betrayal
For Times of War
For Worry-Warts
To Wake Up Those Who Are Sleep-Walking Through Life
For Those Who Have Difficulty Sleeping or Resting
For Meaning and Connection in Place of Boredom and Loneliness
For Peace Amidst the Busy-ness of Life
For Those Who Wait
For Those with Addictions
For Those Facing Death or Major Changes in Life
At the Serious Illness or Death of a Pet or Other Creature in Your Midst
In Honor of Pear Trees Called Peary and Percy
For Changes in a Woman's Ministry (Lay or Ordained)
For Church Leaders
To "The Three Most Sacred" from *Women's Uncommon Prayers: Our Lives Revealed, Nurtured, Celebrated,* eds. Elizabeth Rankin Geitz, Marjorie A. Burke, and Ann Smith (Harrisburg, PA.: Morehouse Publishing, 2000), 38.

Patricia wrote these:

For Cooking
For Giving Goods to Charity
For Those Considering Separation or Divorce
On Splitting the Blanket
For Those in Need of Healing the Wounded Modern Masculine or Eternal Feminine
For Those Assimilating Mystic Experience

From Part Four

Jane researched and put together the calendar with suggestions from Patricia. Jane also researched and wrote all of the Collects for the Mystics, Saints, and Other Extraordinary Folk, Events, and Gifts of Creation.

From Part Five

Jane with Patricia's help wrote the Services of Beginnings:

- A Ritual of Welcoming
- A Ritual of Joining except for Patricia's Invocation listed below

Jane wrote A Rite to Redeem Eden's Goodness.

Jane wrote these parts of the Services of Transformation:

- A Service of Healing: Prayers and procedure for The Flower Ritual
- A Service of Reconciliation: Procession with a Parasol of Paradise
  - Prayers for the followers of the religions of the world
  - Prayers for Living in Harmony with Creation with Patricia's help

Patricia wrote these parts of the Services of Transformation:

- A Ritual of Joining: Invocation of the Archangels
- A Service of Healing: Song of the Bear Matron to her Cubs: A Catechesis
  - Prayers of the Community—The Litany for Martyrs and Those Who Have Suffered Violence
- A Service of Reconciliation: Patricia's Version of the Traditional Beauty Way Chant
- A Labyrinth Service

From Part Six

For Crafts for Use during the Services, Jane wrote the Instructions on Be-Ribboning a Teether for A Ritual of Welcoming and Making a Parasol of Paradise for A Service of Reconciliation. Jane researched and wrote the Table of the Religions of the World.

Patricia researched and wrote the Table of Animals, Plants, and Minerals used in the Weekly Collects. For Crafts for Use during the Services, Patricia wrote the Instructions on Making Prayersticks for A Ritual of Joining (plus other special occasions).

Drawer Five

BIBLIOGRAPHY OF TRANSLATIONS OF WORKS CITED FROM ANCIENT SOURCES

Although St. Ephrem's works are usually cited by the Latin titles in Beck's volumes, Jane used their English titles in this book and gives her English references here with the Latin ones under Beck below. Jane Richardson Jensen translated the following excerpts from the Hebrew, Syriac, and/or Greek:

Mekhilta of Rabbi Ishmael's Bahodesh 5.IX
Odes of Solomon 19; 28:1–2
Acts of Judas Thomas, Act II, ¶142; Act V, ¶50
Macarian Homily 27 and
The following Hymns by St. Ephrem the Syrian:
Hymns of Faith 10.5–6, 17; 62.10; 74.9
Hymns of Nativity 4.149–50, 153–154; 6.13; 9.7–16, 13.7; 21.12; 27.15, 19–20
Hymns of Church 25.18; 30.1
Songs of Nisibis 14.11, 16
Hymns of Virginity 6.8; 22.2, 4, 6–8, 12–13, 20–21; 23.1, 4–7; 24.7; 25.2–3, 9, 15–16; 26.9; 33.1; 51.1
Hymns of Resurrection 1.7 and
Sermons of our Lord 53

For the original languages, commentary, translations, and aids, see:

Beck, Edmund, ed. *Corpus Scriptorum Christianorum Orientalium* (Louvain, Belgium)
Hymnen De Fide, Vol. 154, Scriptores Syri 73 (1955)
Hymnen De Nativitate, Vol. 186, Scriptores Syri 82 (1959)
Hymnen De Eccelsia, Vol. 198, Scriptores Syri 84 (1960)
Carmina Nisibena, Vol. 218, Scriptores Syri 92 (1961)
Hymnen De Virginitate, Vol. 23, Scriptores Syri 94 (1962)
Paschahymnen (De Resurrectione), Vol. 248, Scriptores Syri 108 (1964)
Sermo De Domino Nostro, Vol. 270, Scriptores Syri 116 (1966).

Berthold, Heinz, ed. *Reden und Briefe (von) Makarios/Symeon. Die Sammlung I des Vaticanus Graecus 694 (B)* (Berlin: Akademie-Verlag, 1973).

Brown, Francis, S. R. Driver, Charles A. Briggs. *A Hebrew and English Lexicon of the Old Testament.* Repr. 1906. Repr., Oxford: Clarendon Press, 1951.

Charlesworth, James Hamilton, ed./tr. *The Odes of Solomon.* Oxford: Clarendon Press, 1973.

Jensen, Jane Richardson. "Father, Son, and Holy Spirit as Mothers in Early Syrian Literature." *Continuum* 2, Nos. 2 and 3 (1993): 27–49.

Klostermann, Erich, and Heinz Berthold. *Neue Homilien. Texte und Untersuchungen* 72 (Berlin: Akademie-Verlag, 1961).

Lauterbach, Jacob Z. *Mekhilta de-Rabbi Ishmael. II.* 1933. Repr., Philadelphia: The Jewish Publication Society of America, 1976.

McVey, Kathleen. *St. Ephrem the Syrian Hymns.* Mahwah, N.Y.: Paulist Press, 1989.

Richardson, Jane E. "Feminine Images of the Holy Spirit in the Hymns of St. Ephrem the Syrian." Ph.D. diss., University of Edinburgh, Scotland, 1991.

———. "Mekhilta of Rabbi Ishmael's Bahodesh 5–8 (The Ten Commandments)." M. A. thesis, University of Texas at Austin, December 1985.

Smith, J. Payne (Mrs. Margoliouth), ed. *A Compendious Syriac Dictionary: Founded upon the Thesaurus Syriacus of R. Payne Smith.* 1903. Repr., Oxford: Clarendon Press, 1985.

Wright, W., ed. "The Acts of Judas Thomas" in *Apocryphal Acts of the Apostles.* London & Edinburgh: Williams & Norgate, 1871.

Drawer Six

GENERAL BIBLIOGRAPHY

Bauman, Lynn C. *A Handbook to Practical Wisdom.* Telephone, Tex.: PRAXIS: The Contemplative Christian Tradition, n.d.

Cotter, Jim. "An Alternative Lord's Prayer," as originally written.

Holy Bible with Apocrypha, New Revised Standard Version. Oxford, N.Y.: Oxford University Press, 1989.

Jensen, Jane Richardson. "The Three Most Sacred," in *Women's Uncommon Prayers: Our Lives Revealed, Nurtured, Celebrated.* Edited by Elizabeth Rankin Geitz, Marjorie A. Burke, and Ann Smith. Harrisburg, Pa.: Morehouse Publishing, 2000.

Keller, Helen. "Humble Tasks," in *The Treasure Chest.* Edited by Charles L. Wallis. New York: Harpers and Row, 1965.

Kraft, William F. *Sexual Dimensions of the Celibate.* Dublin: Gill and Macmillan, 1979.

Lesko, Barbara S., ed. *Women's Earliest Records From Ancient Egypt and Western Asia.* Atlanta, Ga.: Scholars Press, 1989.

Motlmann-Wendel, Elisabeth and Jurgen Moltmann. *Humanity in God.* London: SCM Press, Ltd., 1983.

Murray, Robert. *Symbols of Church and Kingdom: A Study in Early Syriac Tradition.* London: Cambridge University Press, 1975.

Schuon, Frithjof. *Transcendent Unity of Religions.* Wheaton, Ill.: Theosophical House, 1993.

Stewart, Julia. *African Proverbs and Wisdom.* New York: Dafina Books, 1997.

For the Table of Religions

Adler, Margot. *Drawing Down the Moon.* New York: Penguin Compass, 1986.

Anderson, Bernhard W. *Understanding the Old Testament.* 4th ed., 1957. Repr., Englewood, N.J.: Prentice-Hall, 1986.

Beversluis, Joel, ed. *A Sourcebook for Earth's Community of Religions.* Rev. ed. Grand Rapids, Mich.: CoNexus Press with Global Education Associates, 1995.

Bowker, John. *Oxford Dictionary of World Religions.* Oxford, N.Y.: Oxford University Press, 1997.

———. *World Religions.* London: Dorling Kindersley Limited, 1997.

Smith, Huston. *The Illustrated World's Religions.* San Francisco: Harper Collins, 1994.

For Patricia's Collects and Correlations

Andrews, Ted. *Animal-Speak: The Spiritual and Magical Powers of Creatures Great and Small.* St. Paul, Minn.: Llewellyn Publications, 1993.

———. *Animal-Wise: The Spirit Language and Signs of Nature.* Jackson, Tenn.: Dragonhawk Publishing, 1999.

"Deciduous Shrubs." Cited 22–25 July 2003. Online: www.paghat.com/garden13.html.

"Gemstone Symbolism." Cited 22–25 July 2003. Online: www.annemeplon.com/meaning.htm.

Greenway, Kate. *The Language of Flowers.* 1885.

Kidwell, Clara Sue, Homer Noley, and George E. Tinker. "Tink." *A Native American Theology.* Maryknoll, N.Y.: Orbis Books, 2001.

McGaa, Ed. *Mother Earth Spirituality: Native American Paths to Healing Ourselves and Our World.* San Francisco, Calif.: HarperCollins, 1990.

Sams, Jamie, and David Carson. *Medicine Cards, Revised, Expanded Edition.* New York: St. Martin's, 1999 [1988].

Sams, Jamie. *Sacred Path Cards: The Discovery of Self through Native Teachings.* San Francisco: HarperCollins, 1990.

Bottom Drawer

BIBLIOGRAPHY FOR THE PEOPLE AND EVENTS ON THE CHURCH CALENDAR

Although all of the Collects from Part Four are Jane's, the people and events in the Church Calendar were drawn from the following sources. Jane intentionally used a variety of sources, some especially written for girls, to make this book accessible to females of any age.

A. A. General Service Conference-approved Literature. "The Co-Founders of Alcoholics Anonymous: Biographical sketches. Their last major talks." Pamphlet. Repr., New York: The A. A. Grapevine, Inc., 1975.

Al-Anon Family Groups. "Al-Anon's Co-Founders, The Extraordinary Work of Two Ordinary Women." Pamphlet. Virginia Beach, Va.: Al-Anon Family Group Headquarters, Inc., n.d.

Anderson, Loraine. *Sisters of the Earth.* 2nd ed. New York: Vintage Books, 2003.

Anderson, Owanah. *400 Years: Anglican/Episcopal Mission Among American Indians.* Cincinnati, Ohio: Forward Movement Publications, 1997.

Appiah, Kwame Anthony, and Henry Louis Gates, Jr., eds. *The Africana Encyclopedia of the African and African-American Experience.* Philadelphia: Running Press, 2003.

Bolden, Tonya, ed. *33 things every girl should know about women's history.* New York: Crown Publishers, 2002.

Chester, Pamela, and Sibelan Forrester, eds. *Engendering Slavic Literature.* Bloomington: Indiana University Press, 1996.

Deen, Edith. *All of the Women of the Bible.* New York: Harper & Row, 1955.

———. *Great Women of the Christian Faith.* New York: Harper & Brothers, 1959.

Delaney, John J. *Dictionary of Saints.* New York: Doubleday, 1980.

Echols, Anne, and Marty Williams, eds. *An Annotated Index of Medieval Women.* New York: Markus Wiener Publishing, 1992.

Efimov, Nina A., Christine D. Tomei, and Richard L. Chapple, eds. *Critical Essays on the Prose and Poetry of Modern Slavic Women.* Lewiston, N.Y.: The Edwin Mellen Press, 1998.

Ellsberg, Robert. *All Saints: Daily Reflections on Saints, Prophets, and Witnesses for our Time.* New York: Crossroad, 1997.

Keller, Helen. *The Story of My Life.* New York: Bantam Books, 1988.

Klapthor, Margaret Brown. *The First Ladies.* 10th ed. Contributing author Allida M. Brown. Washington, D.C.: White House Historical Association, 2001.

The Lesbian Almanac. Compiled by the National Museum and Archive of Lesbian and Gay History. New York: Berkeley Books, 1996.

Lyman, Darryl. *Great African-American Women.* New York: Gramercy Books, 1999.

Mullane, Deirdre, ed. *Crossing the Danger Water: Three Hundred Years of African-American Writing.* New York: Anchor Books, 2003.

O'Ceirin, Kit, and Cyril O'Ceirin. *Women of Ireland: A Biographic Dictionary.* Newtownlynch: Tir Eolas, 1996.

Parbury, Kathleen. *Women of Grace: A Biographical Dictionary of British Women Saints, Martyrs and Reformers.* Stocksfield, England: Oriel Press, 1985.

Peterson, Barbara Bennett, Guanghu Zhang, et al, eds. *Notable Women of China: Shang Dynasty to the Early Twentieth Century.* Armonk, N.Y.: M. E. Sharpe, 2000.

RavenWolf, Silver. *To Light A Sacred Flame.* St. Paul, Minn.: Llewellyn Publications, 1991.

Ruether, Rosemary Radford. *Women-Church: Theology and Practice of Feminist Liturgical Communities.* San Francisco: Harper & Row, 1985.

Stoutenburgh, Jr., John. *Dictionary of the American Indian.* New York: Wings Books, 1990.

Strong, Kenneth. *Ox Against the Storm: A Biography of Tanaka Shozo—Japan's Conservationist Pioneer.* Kent: Japan Library, 1995.

Summers, Lucy. *The Book of Wicca.* Hauppauge, N.Y.: Barron's, 2003.

Towill, Edwin Sprott. *Saints of Scotland.* Edinburgh: Saint Andrew Press, 1994.

Waldman, Carl, ed. *Biographical Dictionary of American Indian History to 1900.* Rev. ed. New York: Checkmarks, 2001.

Walker, Barbara G., ed. *The Woman's Encyclopedia of Myths and Secrets.* San Francisco: Harper & Row,1983.

Ward, Geoffrey C., and Ken Burns. *Not for Ourselves Alone: The Story of Elizabeth Cady Stanton and Susan B. Anthony.* New York: Alfred A. Knopf, 1999, based on a PBS documentary by Ken Burns and Paul Barnes.

Women in History. Rachel Carson Biography. Cited 15 October 2003. Online: www.lkwdpl.org/wihohio/cars-rac.htm.

For an entry on the Church Calendar only, no Collect written:

"Ambedkar, Bhimrao Ramji." Cited 6 January 2004. Online: www.web.net/~acjp/acjpambedkar.html.

Babcock, Michael. *Goddesses Knowledge Cards.* Rohnert Park, Calif.: Pomegranate, n. d.).

Bowker, John. *Oxford Dictionary of World Religions.* Oxford, N.Y.: Oxford University Press, 1997.

Dietrich, Amy, et al. *Great Women and Why Your Daughter Should Know Who They Are.* White Plains, N.Y.: Peter Pauper Press, Inc., 1998.

Franck, Irene, and David Brownstone, eds. *The Women's Desk Reference.* New York: Viking, 1993.

"Hamilton, Alice." *Encyclopaedia Britannica.* 2003. Cited 7 December 2003. Online: www.britannica.com/ed/article?eu=39837.

"Meir, Golda." *Colliers Encyclopedia CD-ROM.* Cited 8 January 2004. Online: www.ou.org/chagim/yomhaatmauth/golda.html.

Moura, Ann (Anoumiel). *Green Witchcraft: Folk Magic, Fairy Lord, and Herb Craft.* St. Paul, Minn.: Llewellyn Publications, 2003.

Olsen, James S. *Bathsheba's Breast: Women, Cancer, and History.* Baltimore : The Johns Hopkins University Press, 2002.

Price, A. Whigham. *The Ladies of Castlebrae.* London: Headline, 1985.

Q., Joe. "Lori Ann Piestewa's Legacy."*Native Web.* Native Web Resources for Indigenous Cultures around the World. Cited 6 January 2004. Online: www.nativeweb.org/weblog/piestewa/.

Reader, John. *A Biography of the Continent of Africa.* New York: Vintage Books, 1999.

Unknown. "Ellen Swallow Richards." Cited 7 December 2003. Online: www.curie.che.virginia.edu/scientist/richards.html.

Unknown. "Mister Rogers dies at age 74—Feb. 27, 2003." Cited 6 January 2004. Online: www.cnn.com/2003/SHOWBIZ/TV/02/27rogers.obit.

Unknown. "Sister Ignatia Gavin and A.A./St. Thomas Hospital." Cited 3 October 2003. Online: www.silkworth.net/aahistory/Ignatia.html.

Webb, Gisela, ed. *Windows of Faith: Muslim Women Scholar-Activists in North America.* Syracuse, N.Y.: Syracuse University Press, 2000.